CW01304846

Literature of Marginality
Dalit Literature
and
African-American
Literature

Literature of Marginality
Dalit Literature and African-American Literature

edited by
N.M. ASTON
**Reader and Head
Department of English
Nowrosjee Wadia College
Pune**

PRESTIGE

PRESTIGE BOOKS
3/28, East Patel Nagar
New Delhi 110 008

All rights reserved. No part of this book may be reproduced or transmitted in any form or by any means, electronic or mechanical including photocopying, recording or any information storage or retrieval system, without prior permission in writing from the editor

© Editor, 2001

ISBN: 81-7551-116-8

Printed at Chaman Offset Press, New Delhi 110 002

Contents

Introduction
N.M. Aston
9

Literature of Marginality
J.M. Waghmare
16

**Dalit Literature and African-American Literature:
A Comparative Study**
R. Bhongle
25

Some Reflections on Dalit Literature
R.G. Jadhav
37

Dalit Literature: A Historical Background
M.D. Nalavade
41

Dalit Literature: A Minority Discourse
V.D. Phadke
55

Dalit Poetry
L.S. Deshpande
59

**Treatment of Women in the
Fiction of Anna Bhau Sathe**
S.D. Khandagale
73

**The Theme of Marginality in
Anna Bhau Sathe's Novels and Short Stories**
B.S. Korde
83

**Awakening Social Consciousness:
Mulk Raj Anand's *Untouchable***
R.K. Dhawan
93

**The Crisis in Human Values in
Mulk Raj Anand's *Coolie* and
Arundhati Roy's *The God of Small Things*:
A Comparative Study**
Rosy Misra
110

**Black Identity in
Selected Novels of William Faulkner**
K.S. Iyer
119

Motherhood in Toni Morrison's *Beloved*
Bharati A. Parikh
127

**The Theme of Marginality in
Toni Morrison's *The Bluest Eye***
J. Salve
137

**Towards a Minority Poetics:
A Critique of Binarism and Marginalism in
Paule Marshall's Texts**
H. Kulkarni
144

Dedicated to
all those
who have suffered and are suffering
neglect, inhumanity and injustice
at the hands of their own brethren

CONTRIBUTORS

N.M. ASTON	Nowrosjee Wadia College, Pune
R. BHONGLE	University of Bombay, Mumbai
L.S. DESHPANDE	People's College, Nanded
R.K. DHAWAN	S.B.S. College, University of Delhi
K.S. IYER	T.C. College, Baramati
R.G. JADHAV	Pune
S.D. KHANDAGALE	S.P. College, Pune
B.S. KORDE	University of Pune, Pune
H. KULKARNI	S.R.T. Marathwada University, Nanded
ROSY MISRA	Govt. M.K.B. College, Jabalpur
M.D. NALAVADE	Former Professor of History and Registrar, University of Pune, Pune
BHARATI A. PARIKH	M.S.G. University, Vadodara
V.D. PHADKE	Fergusson College, Pune
J. SALVE	Nowrosjee Wadia College, Pune
B.S. KORDE	University of Pune, Pune
J.M. WAGHMARE	Former Vice-Chancellor, S.R.T. Marathwada University, Nanded

Introduction

N.M. ASTON

I

The theme 'Literature of Marginality' on which the articles in this book are focussed, relates to literature produced to project the juggernaut of social, religious and casteist oppression under which the dalits of India and the blacks in Africa and some parts of America eke out their too heavy a burden of life.

The causes and circumstances leading to the age-old existence of oppression and despair of the lives of the marginalised class of nation's vast majority of people can be enumerated thus:

1. The self down-gradation of these people since ages, suppressing even the slightest protest against injustice that sought to find a voice.
2. The conditions of abject poverty, unhealthy and insanitary conditions in which these people had been sheltered, but they held a belief that they were accursed to live such lives.
3. Even the minimum rights as human beings denied to them, rendering them incapable of seeing the light of freedom and comfortable living, thanks to the age-old ideology taught to them by the upper castes in India and the white race in other countries, that they were fated to be hewers of wood and drawers of water—mere slaves!
4. The portals of education were never opened for them to taste the power of freedom.

The literature that was produced by writers, who themselves had experienced at first hand, the oppression and segregation, issued out of the cores of their bleeding hearts. The literature of the marginalised community attracted attention of readers, both of the downtrodden and the well-placed sections, by their profoundness and veracity. In course of time, through works of Anna Bhau Sathe in India and Baldwin Wright, Toni Morrison and others in the western world, a new poetics of the oppressed classes emerged distinctly. It was, and continues to be even today, the poetics of liberation. The need is, now, to fulfil a long-cherished and much deserved liberation of the downtrodden through education and through legislation. The social process of regeneration that has been set in motion by the literature produced by the oppressed, for the oppressed, has had a salutary result, namely that of creating an awareness, among the oppressed about the need to rise above their line of least resistance and to claim their right to live with honour.

Legislation and the process of reorientation of the social system have begun to yield results. But the damage done over the years cannot be compensated overnight. The battle for rights has begun and the new dawn of freedom and equality is appearing in the sky, though darkened by sporadic incidents of oppression in some quarters still occurring.

II

In his article 'Literature of Marginality' J.M. Waghmare regards 'marginality' as a term applicable universally to the peoples of the world living in conditions of abject poverty and as a consequence isolated from the mainstream life. The blacks in other countries and the dalits belong to this marginalised group. Inequality of all kinds resulting from insecurity, injustice and exploitation consigned them to their deplorable fate. With changing times, with educational opportunities afforded to them, their conditions are improving but still they face the question of regaining their identity. The Indian Dalit writing emerging as a powerful voice claiming the rightful place for the Dalits, and standing out as a new poetics of Dalits, redefining the identity of the dalits which in recent times has included dalit women's rights as an indispensable condition for dalit independence and equality, exploding the myth of marginality, is a decisive step in this direction.

Rangarao Bhongle in his article on "Literature of Marginality—Dalit Literature and African-American Literature: A Comparative Study" holds the view that Dalit and African-American literatures are not 'marginal' but 'mainstream' literatures by virtue of their focus on the fundamental questions of human life, which embraces every cross-section of civilized society. Ironically enough, even the language, idiom and dialect employed in the writings of this literature is the mainstream English, dispossessing the elitist claims to English. The article refers to seminal and germinal works to establish his contention. Dr. Bongle's thesis is that Dalit and African-American literatures, in their respective societies do not subvert, but create new canons of writing.

R.G. Jadhav in his article entitled, 'Some Reflections on Dalit Literature' considers Dalit Literature as the nativistic, postcolonial movement aimed at the cultivation of creative urges of the downtrodden masses, thanks to the rigid Indian caste system. He argues that Dalit literature focuses attention on fundamental human values to reestablish secular values like individuality, identity, liberty, equality, fraternity, which were for long eschewed in their context. Initially, Dalit literature began as a voice of protest against an unjust social order. Today, it has attained the status of a distinct, creative world literature reflecting the plight of the majority people of the world, and highlighting the struggle of the human spirit against age-old oppressions.

M.D. Nalavade's in his article 'Dalit Literature: A Historical Background' conducts a succinct historical survey of Dalit literature in India in various states. He opines that ancient Hindu literature was conspicuously Brahmanic and excluded a vast majority of India. He draws attention to the inherent lacunae in *Manusmriti* which excluded Dalits, whereas the Shudras derived their origin from the solar race, as Dr. Ambedkar's research revealed. Dr. Nalawade affirms that Dr. Ambedkar has been the apostle of the dalits and toeing his line Dalit writers began to write focusing on themes such as disabilities imposed upon dalits, demand of social equality, social justice, Buddhism and social and economic democracy. Today, Dalit writers, inspired by Anna Bhau Sathe have left their indelible mark on the literature of India.

In his article entitled 'Dalit Literature: A Minority Discourse' Vivekanand Phadke dismantles the age-old term 'Dalit' as applied to the marginalised Maharashtrian underdogs by arguing, that it is a misnomer to call them 'Marginal' when they are numerically the majority. He opines that the successive onslaughts at the fortress of Dalits by the actual minority Sadashivpeth culture was the cause of the relegation of the Dalits. He argues that the future emergence of the Dalit as the true representative of Maharashtrian social culture depends largely on the need to evolve an idiom of their own as well as the possibility of neo-capitalism doing away with the existing caste hierarchy.

L.S. Deshpande in his article on 'Dalit Poetry' conducts a brief survey of Dalit Poetry upholding the poetry in Marathi of the Dalits as a protest against the establishment, as an augury and a commitment towards ushering a new order with new values. He argues that Dalit poetry, playing as it does on the delicate heartstrings of Dalit sensibility with its themes of morality, basic life, mother image, new consciousness, physical and spiritual hunger, individual dignity vis-à-vis society, Buddhism as a salvation for the demented Dalit Soul, love of India and so on, is calculated to blaze the torch for a new era for Mankind, a 'brave new world' bereft of suffering, suppression and exploitation, with the stigma of Dalit, no more a scourge.

S.D. Khandagale, in his article 'Treatment of Women in the Fiction of Anna Bhau Sathe' holds the view that the four-fold caste system in India denigrated women to the lowest and fourth category alongside Shudras, and *Manusmriti* rendered their plight worse than that of slaves. Through his fiction Anna Bhau Sathe projects women as strong, self-respecting and of good moral character, thereby equating them with men and even elevating them to a model of sacrifice and selflessness, worth emulation even by men. Anna Bhau Sathe gives them names such as Sandalwood, Lotus in the Mud etc. He was, undoubtedly, the first in championing the cause of Feminism in India, not by following the Western Feminism which upheld socially superior and well placed women, but by evolving a new image of woman from among the downtrodden.

B.S. Korde (who has authored a book on Anna Bhau Sathe) in his article entitled 'The Theme of Marginality in Anna Bhau Sathe's Novels and Short Stories' argues that Anna Bhau Sathe's works dealing with the downtrodden classes project the theme, not of submission and fatality but of putting up a brave front to write a new chapter of their rightful place in society by reordering the caste-ridden society into recognising the worth of the erstwhile downtrodden, so-called marginalised. The article deals with Anna Bhau Sathe's famous path-breaking works which prove that often, truth is stranger than fiction where the tenacity of the downtrodden to eke out a living is concerned.

Mulk Raj Anand is a novelist with a social purpose. In his scholarly article 'Awakening Social Consciousness: Mulk Raj Anand's *Untouchable*', R.K. Dhawan points out that a close study of Anand's works shows that he juxtaposes the social evils against the mindsets of individuals and some privileged sections of the society. In *Untouchable*, he deals with the ghastly evil of untouchability afflicting the Hindu society of the pre-Partition era, in the larger backdrop of the caste-configurations within the Hindu society that have successfully stifled the healthy growth of a considerable section of Indian community for centuries. A strong believer in the dignity of man and equality of all men, Anand is naturally shocked by the inhuman way the untouchables are treated by those that belong to superior castes—especially the Brahmins or the so-called "twice-born." Towards the end of the novel, Anand suggests a few solutions to the evil of untouchability.

Arundhati Roy has emerged as a prophetess of the new millennium. In her article 'The Crisis in Human Values in Mulk Raj Anand's *Coolie* and Arundhati Roy's *The God of Small*

Things: A Comparative Study', Rosy Misra points out that the two novels are comparable on various levels. Both are revolutionary novels and depict the social reality of conflict between the powerful and the powerless, and treat the downtrodden humanistically.

K.S. Iyer's article 'Black Identity in Selected Novels of William Faulkner', considers the three novels, *Absalom, Absalom! Intruder in the Dust* and *The Sound and the Fury* as a trilogy encompassing a vast historical period in American history of racialism, starting from the Civil war to the eve of the Great Depression of 1929-30. During the course of this one and a half centuries and odd years, Faulkner has shown the positive change from hatred and dehumanization of the Negro race in the Civil War period to the end of 1920s when in *The Sound and the Fury* we have Dilsey the Negro servant, who through suffering, forgiveness, sacrifice and religiosity attains to a state of spiritual ascension, in which the differences between the two races appear to have been totally submerged, prophesying, as it were, the equality with, and identity of the Negro race as, human beings.

In her article, 'Motherhood in Toni Morrison's *Beloved*' Bharati Parikh explores the concept of 'motherhood' the novelist propounds in the backdrop of the life of plantation workers during the plantation and slavery era. Morrison projects the 'mother' as a Negro-archetypal-cum-ancestral concept who slaved with her heart and soul and stood out as an 'unchurched' preacher extolling the pricelessness of the 'heart' and the 'soul' in the mother, which no civilization, however, inhuman, can scrape them out of their bodies. Such was the 'sterner stuff' Sethe was made of! Sethe symbolised the archetypal Negro-woman who suffered for the race and she was 'the race' itself, transcending physical barriers beyond the region of physical pain.

Jayant Salve in his article on 'The Theme of Marginality in Toni Morrison's *The Bluest Eye*' argues that the tragedy of the black Americans lies in their rootlessness resulting from their senseless striving to initiate themselves into the American white society by desiring to equal American standard of beauty, such as blue eyes, as Pecola in the novel prays for, fervently. The black Americans find themselves relegated to a class of marginalised both by deserting their own class and by being stranded ruthlessly, into the resultant hell of neglect for imitating white standards of beauty for acceptance on levels of equality. Harihar Kulkarni in his article 'Towards a Minority Poetics: A Critique of Binarism and Marginalism in Paule Marshall's Texts," argues that the need has arisen, today to 'decode' and 'de-mystify' the banality of marginality so as to reorder and bring into being a society where there exists an 'aesthetics of balance and harmony'. This will be a new minority poetics as envisaged by Paule Marshall, who in the Sixties sought to evolve textual strategies in which the binarism of patriarchal and colonial hegemony will stand totally displaced or decapitated.

III

I must express my sincere thanks and gratitude to Dr. R.K. Dhawan of University of Delhi who helped me in the preparation and publication of the book. I am grateful to Professor K.S. Iyer, my mentor, who has been a constant source of inspiration in bringing out the book. I would be failing in my duty if I do not record my gratitude to Dr. B.S. Korde, Prof. S.D. Khandagale and Dr. Suman Bala who acted like the spirit behind the scene in bringing out the book. Finally, I express my appreciation and gratitude to Prestige Books for publishing this book expeditiously and so elegantly.

Literature of Marginality

J.M. WAGHMARE

These days we have been discussing the problems of marginalised groups of people all over the world—their social, ethnic, economic and cultural problems. Marginality with all its aspects is indeed a major problem to be reckoned with in the world.

By and large, most of the marginalised groups, if not all, constitute minorities—religious, ethnic, linguistic or otherwise—in different countries. They have sub-cultures in this mainstream cultures or religions. Invariably, they are impoverished people constituting of minority groups. They suffer from economic, social or political impoverishment and find themselves estranged from this mainstream. Their marginality may vary in its degree, extent or intensity. Most countries and cultures have empowered groups at one pole and impoverished groups at the other and between the two, the people having graded power and poverty. The empowered people enjoy greater degree of freedom, social status and security of life. The impoverished people are not free from fear, insecurity and injustice. The form and nature of marginality depends upon the degree of impoverishment—economic, social or cultural. Marginality based upon caste, creed, religion or race is a kind of disability or affliction.

What is the root cause of marginality? I think inequality is the main cause of marginality. Inequality is a source of insecurity, injustice and exploitation. Marginalised sections of society are generally beyond the pale of the dominant culture. Their existence is, by and large, peripheral. All cultures and societies, advanced or disadvanced, have power centres in their corpus.

The marginalised groups or sections are consciously or unconsciously distanced from the power centres. They are scattered here and there and lack cohesiveness and strength. Deprived of economic, political or religious power, as they are, they grope in the dark for survival. They live in physical or psychological ghettos. The social organisation in which they are imprisoned by custom and tradition builds walls of segregation around them. However, they struggle for emancipation.

But the times are changing. Democracy all over the world has given all such marginal groups of people an opportunity to share freedom with their compatriots. It has made them aware of their human rights and civil liberties. They enjoy the right of franchise, which is a political weapon. Education and freedom of expression give voice to the voiceless. The death of colonialism has given birth to political awareness and freedom creating thereby aspirations in the minds of the people for attaining equal status and dignity. However, there are sections of people who are deprived of equal opportunity, equal social status and equal individual dignity. Naturally, they express their concerns, anxieties and anguishes in their writing. 'Who are we?' 'What is our future?' 'What is our status?' etc. Questions like these haunt their minds. They have a quest for their identity. Yes, identity is their problem. Dreams they have and nightmares they confront. They explore their past and struggle for their future. They excavate their long past to trace the fossils of their forefathers's existence and also forge their future. Their literature is indeed a creative excavation for their heritage.

Let me take up the literature of two marginalised groups of people for brief discussions namely, the American Blacks and the Indian Dalits. The blacks in America and the dalits in India are the marginalised and exploited people, their marginality being primarily social and economic. We hear their protest voices in their literatures. The black American asks a pertinent question to Providence in his baritone:

What did I do
To be so black

And blue?

He is condemned because he is black. Nature is responsible for that. What it means to be a black man in this world dominated by the white race? The black American writer defines his racial condition which is responsible, by and large, for his sociocultural condition in the conspiring world of the white people. Suffering is indeed his lot. He has committed no sin. Nobody has however, talked about the Black Adam's fall. Nor has anybody applied the Indian doctrine of Karma to his socio-racial conditions to explain his perpetual suffering, torture and trauma for being black. Was it preordained by some invisible power? The Karma doctrine can be applied to only individuals, men or women, but not to the whole race—black, brown or white.

As you know, a very cruel slavery was imposed on the blacks in America for more than three centuries. The land of liberty locked them in this dark dungeon of slavery. Their racial problem resulted into social, economic and cultural problems. The inhuman exploitation of the American blacks has no parallel in the history of mankind. The slavery was institutionalised in the social behaviour. The white people gave bad treatment to the Negro as per the code ingrained in the minds of both the white and black people. The black race was marginalised in all respects. The shackles of slavery fell only after the Civil War. But they were not shattered completely. The Jim Crow laws were passed to put them in bondage. The highest court of America upheld the notorious 'separate-but-equal' principle. The Negro was defranchised. Benefit of legal power and property, he was ditched into troubled waters. Slavery was 'a peculiar institution'.

Freedom without bread is meaningless. The blacks felt that slavery with bread was better than freedom without bread. But it was also true that bread with slavery is a poisoned bread. The option before them was obvious and clear. They chose freedom because it gave them strength to struggle. "All men were created equal'. This was the corner-stone of the American Constitution. Here 'all men' did not include "black men'. That was the unfortunate reality. Or surreality? The American blacks have fought long legal battles in American courts to affirm their rights.

America always cherished the dream of liberty, equality and happiness. These are the irreducible and inalienable rights of the citizens of the U.S.A. They are guaranteed by the Constitution. But often they were violated. The American Dream remained illusive. American blacks also preserved that dream under their heavy swollen eyelids and held it tightly between their thick bleeding lips. But it was snatched from them time and again. This racial dilemma remained unresolved. The black American was caught between the American Dream and the American Dilemma. What it means to be an American Negro is a perplexing problem entangling him into a predicament. Black literature is concerned with this situation.

Dalits in India constitute a major marginalised group of people. They were untouchables in this most ancient land of dreams and nightmares, reveries and hallucinations. Untouchability was the result of the travesty of the *Varna Vyavastha* in India. It was a kind of socio-religious slavery imposed upon the dalit people. It got institutionalised over the centuries in social norms, customs and traditions. It however, became a universal and all-pervading phenomenon. The caste Hindus outcast them and pushed them beyond the periphery of Hindu religion and culture. The Indian Dalit laments as though in anguish and anger

> What did I do
> To be so outcast

And though it was always a cry in the wilderness, it echoes today in Dalit literature.

The uppermost of the high caste Hindus apotheosised themselves, dehumanising at the same time the untouchables. Their marginalisation was beyond imagination. The untouchability has indeed been 'a peculiar institution' in India throughout her history. For ages together, untouchability has been an Indian dilemma. It is not possible to trace its *raison d'être*. Anthropologists, sociologists and psychologists have not been able to trace its roots. The Hindu society has essentially been "a closed society" without much of ventilation and obstructing air and light.

American blacks as well as Indian dalits were the sons and daughters of darkness journeying through untold sorrows and sufferings. Dalits are the native sons of India. They were the salt and savour of this ancient land. But unfortunately they were disowned by the high caste Hindus for centuries together. Today the Dalit writer asks: What is India to me? An enigmatic land? A dream or a nightmare? Or a puzzling riddle? He is in search of answers to these questions. What it means to be an untouchable or a pariah? He knows very well that his forefathers sprang out from the same womb as the Brahmins. Why then was he rejected by the mother? Why and how? Who is responsible for this inhuman act? His questions are many. They issue forth from what, who, why, and how. The questions he asks seem to be simple but their answers are amazingly complex. Once Dr. Babasaheb Ambedkar told Mahatma Gandhi in a fit of anguish and anger, "Gandhiji, I have no homeland!" The Dalit writer today is trying to answer these questions. Dalit literature, inspired by Dr. Ambedkar's thoughts, is defining and redefining the dalit conditions. His pen is like a sharp axe with which he is cutting the weeds thickly grown over the centuries in this ancient land.

The American Black writer faces the same dilemma. What is America to me? A deep well of sorrow? A land of travail and trauma? But he knows at the same time that his forefathers were brought to America in chains and auctioned on the shores of Atlanta. The black Americans have irrigated the fertile land of liberty with their blood, fears and sweat. The white settlers defiled their women and lynched them to death. The development and progress of America owes a lot to their labour. They increased the fertility of American agricultural land and made it a Cotton King. They strengthened the sinews of American industry too. Their tragic laughter and steaming tears have made America what it is today—a land of crowning glory.

But Africa, the land of his ancestors, cannot altogether disappear from their memories, however faint these might be. Africa occupies a special place in their hearts and souls. Their conscious minds are filled with America but Africa is stuck forever in their psyche. That is the reason why they call themselves Afro-Americans. Their identity has travelled from coloured to Negro, from Negro to Black, from Black to Afro-American and now from Afro-American to African-American. They are full-blooded African-Americans. Their long dark shadows fall across two continents—America and Africa. Their history is a long passage of time telling a tale of two continents. They were thrown out of their own history, faith and culture. African history has given them a full page, but American history has given only a small and narrow margin on its page. However, their tale of two continents is not a midsummer night's dream. It is indeed a story of an endless hallucination of agony. Nevertheless, they have not lost their hope. They regard this endless hallucination of agony as a kind of liberation through which they regenerate their energy. Read Ralph Ellison's *Invisible Man* to understand this. The essence of American black personality is found in their spirituals, Jazz, Blues, poems, plays, short stories and novels. Marginal is their existence. From Richard Wright's *Native Son* to Alex Haley's *Roots*, the Black American literature deals with the essence of black identity caught in perpetual crisis. But of late, it has revealed the core of optimism. 'We shall overcome someday.'

Indian Dalit writing is a post-Independence literary phenomenon. Not that there were no dalit writers writing before Independence. There were, but they were very few. Even in the long past, saints like Chokhamela and Rohidas were expressing their predicament. Their voices were passive. Today we hear loud voices of protest in Dalit writing. Dalit writing today has a lot of sound and fury. Writers like Shankarrao Kharat, Anna Bhau Sathe, Baburao Bagul, Daya Pawar, Namdev Dhasal, Yashwant Manohar and a host of others have caught the attention of readers. Marathi Dalit literature has become a source of inspiration to dalit writers writing in other Indian languages. Marathi dalit writers constitute the vanguard of dalit writers in India. These writers are inspired by Dr. B.R. Amebdkar's thoughts.

Emergence of Dalit literature has a great historical significance in India. It is generic in the sense that all other marginalised and oppressed groups of people are under its sway and sweep. It has struck a keynote awakening their consciousness for forging their identities. It has given ample inspiration and insight to the writers emerging from the tribal and nomadic communities. Writers like Laxman Mane, Laxman Gaikwad, Kishor Kale and Waharu Sonvane are a few outstanding examples. They too ask the same questions. Who are we? What is our place in Indian society and history? Why is our situation so marginal? Where are our roots to be found? Their clamour is not a cry in the wilderness today. Their voices are not passive. They command our attention. They too are in search of their identities. They are however forging their identities in the crucibles of their plays, poems, short stories and novels. Their writings are autobiographies of their communities. A strong feeling of "we-ness" is writ large in their books. This is a peculiar phenomenon to be found in the literature of the marginalised and oppressed groups. There is, on the one hand, the individual who stands for the community of the ethnic group and the community on the other hand for the individual. They are celebrating their heritage in their own idiom. They have their own aesthetics in rustic and rudimentary forms. They are harnessing and developing their own aesthetics. Especially the adivasis have a very rich tradition of dance, music and folklore. They can reconstruct their image and identity on it by way of new interpretations. The American blacks have their own black aesthetic theory. The Indian dalits are trying to develop their own aesthetics mirroring their perceptions of life and the world around. Literature is after all a mirror that reflects the outer world as well as the inner universe. What is more important in the literature of the marginalised groups of people is the social milieu. The creative writer should put the social milieu into the artistic form. An artistic milieu should emerge from his poetry or fiction. He should not get alienated from his own roots and from his own common people. With the rise of middle class, the urge of the writer to give a voice to the common people gets weakened. A black bourgeois class gradually emerged from the black masses. Similarly, a dalit bourgeois class has started emerging from the dalits. Writers who belong to the marginalised groups should not develop the bourgeois mentality. All marginalised groups in India are awakening from their slumber. They are analysing their social conditions. Marginalised groups such as the Indian Muslims and the Indian Christians are developing their own literature in Marathi and other languages. They have established their own literary forums and organising their own literary conferences. They are redefining their identities after fifty years of Independence. They should recast their own images in new moulds.

We are witnessing today an extraordinary spectacle of women's liberation movements all over the world. It is a universal world phenomenon in the sense that it pervades all the countries and cultures, races and religions. In India too, women writers are writing with a feminist view. Numerically women do not constitute a marginal or minority group. We have fifty percent female population in the country. But women here and elsewhere do not enjoy equal status and individual dignity in the male-dominated world. That makes them marginal—socially, politically, sexually and culturally. Their sexual exploitation ultimately leads to social, political and economic exploitation. Women who belong to the weaker sections of society such as Dalits, Adivasis etc. face double exploitation, double inequality and double injustice. Theirs is a double jeopardy. They face degradation and even dehumanistation. Gender is at the base of their marginality. They face domestic violence too. Husbands and wives are unequal partners in family life. One of the best creations of man is the relation or relationship: mother, father, sister, son, daughter, husband, wife and in-laws. This gives some protection to women. Otherwise, women would have been victims of male lust. And yet they suffer a lot at the hands of men. They move under the dark phallic shadow of man's lust. Feminism deals with all these problems. We often talk about women's empowerment. Their empowerment can be achieved only through education, employment and equality.

Women today find themselves in two worlds—the old one is gradually dying and the new one is powerless to be born. There is every danger of miscarriage. The new world should not be a stillborn baby. Women have been standing at the crossroads of history for centuries with tears in their eyes and milk in their breasts. Ours is a man-centered world. Should we make it a woman-centered world? Neither man-centered nor woman-centered, we must build a human-centered world. That is the dream spread across the pages of feminist literature. Kamala Das says:

> Bereft of soul
> My body shall be bare,
> Bereft of body
> My soul shall be bare.

Women writers's concern is woman's bare body and naked soul. The male-dominated world has used religion, culture and social order to keep women in bondage.

As a matter of fact, all marginalised and oppressed groups of people face the problems of human rights violation which ultimately leads to dehumanisation, if it is not resisted and fought ruthlessly.

There is a nexus, though weak, between the dalit problem and the women's problem at least in Indian society. Both the problems are the products of the Chaturvarna. Women too were regarded as Shudras by the Hindu smritis, especially the *Manusmriti*. They were denied access to education. They were not allowed to touch the Vedas. Women were not *dwijas* (twice born) like the Shudras. The aspect has not yet been dealt with in the Indian feminist writing. Women writers have not yet delved deep into the psyche of the male orthodoxy. There is an awakening in Muslim women writers also. Taslima Nasreen is a voice of rebellion.

Dalit Literature and African-American Literature: A Comparative Study

R. BHONGLE

What is Marginality? The term applies to those areas of human interactions and activities which had only peripheral values, which were relegated to and looked upon as irrelevant and insignificant to the mainstream interest, and which appeared occasionally either to entertain or as an object of pity and sympathy in the so-called mainstream literature. The image of an 'untouchable' in Marathi saint poetry, in the writings of Sane Guruji, S.M. Mate etc. and the image of a woman in the entire world literature appear either as an object of the male desire or as an ideal supporter or assistant to the noble cause to which her male counterpart was dedicated. There are several ethnic groups in plural societies like that of USA and the contemporary UK which once were looked upon as 'marginal' but which today in the postmodernist phase, have posed serious challenge to the so-called mainstream activities or rather they themselves have become the mainstream. In England, for example, the voice of the Caribbean, the Asians, the Africans and the woman's roarings are more audible than the traditional voice of the white male. In recent times, the Booker Prize—the greatest literary award in England—was bagged not by Englishmen, but by Nadine Gordimer, the South African, Derek Walcott, the Caribbean and Arundhati Roy the Indian. The concept of Imperial English with capital 'E' has now been marginalised, instead, there are Caribbean English, African English, the way English is spoken in New Zealand and of course Indian English. Within

India itself, there is a variety of Englishes: the English which the teacher of English with CIEFL and IFEL courses from Hyderabad speak, the English spoken by the privileged proud Indians who visit West off and on and look down upon those whose accents do not correspond to the Received Pronunciations (RP) from London and then, there is English spoken by those in India who lack academic training and who have been educated through vernaculars. This dilation, or dilution of the situation has made everything topsy-turvy, upside down. Those who were marginalised have assumed mainstream relevance, and those who were privileged appear to have been marginalised. This is an oncoming phase which is being described as 'postmodern'. It was in 1947 that British historian Arnold Toynbee used the term 'postmodern'. It was in 1947 that the British saw the emergence of a new class which became assertive in the 1950s. The publication of *Look Back in Anger* and *Lucky Jim* in 1954, the concept of 'two cultures' propounded and propagated by C.P. Snow, the spate of immigrants and expatriates from the Third world and several other factors made the modernist concept of arts and life though not obsolete but outdated. The following decades witnessed both in Europe and America and in several nations of the Third World including India dwindling away of the old values because they were charged of catering to the needs of the privileged few. Such terms as 'deconstruction', 'subversion', 'dismantling', 'mapping', 'remapping', 'decanonizing', 'decoding' etc. became the catchwords of literary discussions. Terms like 'Literary Theory', 'Literary Criticism', were replaced by new terms like 'Ideology' and 'Discourse'. The undue value and emphasis laid on 'text' by the modernists and formalists was replaced by the 'context'. Linguistic expertise, formal accomplishment etc. were replaced by the use of dialects and vernaculars which include slang, even obscene words.

Women, perhaps the most oppressed community in the history, swung into action immediately after they started breathing in open air. Today they are not only the most articulate community, but also the keenest on subverting the conventional norms. The example of an Indian woman kissing Prince Charles publicly on his arrival at Indian airport, or that of Monica Lewinsky's confessions to the Starr commission which supplied pornographic accounts to the Sunday newspapers are not just freak events, they speak for mainstream tendencies today all over the world. The use of four-letter words occurs more frequently in the fiction of women writers than in the writings of men. What Shobha De is doing in India cannot be dismissed as popular tricks. Serious women writers in America like Alice Walker, Dennise Morrision etc. demonstrate graphically what used to be most private and personal experience of men and women or between two women. Kamala Das tells everything about "the endless female hungers."

What I am trying to aim at, or lead you to, is the fact that what once used to be called marginal has assumed considerable importance, because it has proved to be full of potentials and with larger relevance to contemporary life and society, African-American literature, which once was opposed as social documentation, not art as in the case of Dalit literature in Maharashtra, is considered as America's national literature today. It explores the meaning of life in America in a way that no white writer has done before.

I shall not go deep into history, but I must mention a few relevant facts of the African-American Literature. "Literature of Slaves" is as old as the history of human civilization. You must have heard of Aesop's stories which were written to console the inflicted souls. Aesop who was a slave in the ancient Greece, toiled for his masters and composed those stories whenever he could find time and inclination to write. African-American literature which has come to the fore in this century is as old as the history of the United States as a nation. The slaves who were brought from Africa to work on the plantations of the white men, sang to themselves the songs of their miseries and spiritual yearnings. These songs which came down from generation to generation in the oral form are known as 'blues'. These blues were the source of inspiration to many poets of the Harlem renaissance of this century including Langston Hughes, Claude

Mackay, Countee Cullen etc. Again, these blues had inspired many composers of jazz music in America during the 1920s.

The first book to be published by a slave in America was *An Evening Thought Salvation by Christ with Penitential Cries* by Jupiter Hammon. It was in the year 1760. Hammon was followed by a delicate girl called Philis Wheatly who not only produced a fair amount of poetry, but also won the attention of George Washington and Thomas Jefferson as well as a number of prominent people in England. Another slave who was employed in the home of president of the University of North Carolina was George Moses Horton who composed poems and published them in 1829. His biography by Richard Walser was published in the 1970s under the title *The Black Poet*. In 1845 an anthology of Black poetry was published in Paris. This book was called *Les Ceneles* and contains poems of those free men of colour who had migrated to France and had come under the influence of Alexander Dumas who encouraged black arts like sculptor, music, painting and poetry in France.

With these brief historical facts, I shall come down to contemporary African-American literature. I shall not dwell much upon the Harlem Renaissance, though an important cultural event in the history of African-Americans, I shall recall hurriedly the 1940s, and 50s when three great Black writers made invaluable contribution to what at that time was called 'Literature of the Blacks in America' and to the American literature in general. *Native Son* by Richard Wright, *Invisible Man* by Ralph Ellison and *Go Tell It on the Mountain* by James Baldwin produced new vistas for mapping racial prejudice through a genre which subverted all the accepted notions about the blacks in America. The three novels not only offer a graphic account of the black life in America during those days but also they are essentially interrelated thematically as well as in their narrative structures.

The three novels are the record of a common experience. They reveal attitudes of the whites towards the blacks and its devastating effects on the psychology of the blacks. They expose what Richard Wright calls, *Bigger Thomas' Behavioristic Pattern* resulting out of frustration and alienation. These novels have as their heroes three adolescent boys dazed by the stark realities at home and the inimical, almost hostile society which they look up to with great expectations. Though the novels have three different stories to narrate, they end up with similar conclusions. Bigger Thomas in Wright's *Native Son* is to be hanged, the invisible anonymous narrator boy in *Invisible Man* and John Grimes in *Go Tell it on the Mountain* has strange visions in which he experiences intense feelings of shame, despair, guilt and fear. Despite being concerned with the same pattern of life, each one of these novels has its own canons of judging the pattern. Richard Wright's protagonist hates the white to the extent of rejoicing the murder of a white girl even though she knows the consequences. The invisible man shrinks back into the hole—'humiliated and crestfallen'. John Grimes' strange vision towards the end of the novel places him somewhere between anger and frustration. The three different stages, in fact, individual efforts on part of the novelists decode the paradigm, hence intrinsically related with each other.

Let me pause here for a while and see if the similar situation exists in Dalit literature. There aren't so powerful Dalit novels as the three novels by black writers. I can recall only one—"Sud" a sort of long story by Baburao Bagul which is a story of woman's noble rage rather than that of Dalit issue. Another novel by Keshav Meshram entitled *Pokhran* deals mainly with stripping the natives of the cultural values by the Aryans when they settled down after the victory over the native tribes in India. *Pokhran* in fact is a very important novel in the context of the entire Dalit reality, but unfortunately not much has been written about it, maybe because it was published at a time when anger and protest were the major trends in Marathi Dalit literature, and *Pokhran* unravels the bitter reality rather artistically, without being loud. Bhimsen Dethe attempted the novel form, so did Sudhakar Gaikwad—and both these writers portray the Dalit reality effectively as they themselves are a part of the life they write about. I have also attempted the novel—one already published in 1987—called *Soma,* another still awaiting publication—I have called the novel *Timirangan Soma* which is a story of a young Dalit boy whose experiences are similar—equally devastating like those of the adolescent heroes of black novels, I have just referred to. The realities in Dalit life and those in the life of the Blacks in America is the same—poverty, ignorance, oppression and the ultimate alienation. Protest, anger, aggression and discord are the outer expressions of the inner reality (there have been quite a few research works on why the dalit youth finds it difficult to cope and adjust with their colleagues.)

The difficulties regarding the literature of marginality till recently was that it remained mostly unread. Not many readers of Marathi literature can claim to have been acquainted at least with major texts of Dalit writings save "Sud" by Baburao Bagul and *Pokhran* or *Shudra* by Sudhakar Gaikwad. Literature of the blacks in America had suffered similar fate till it achieved the glorious status of African-American Literature. It is only recently that the literary canons or the canonical concepts were challenged and the marginalised came to the forefront. Shakespeare, for example, remained an unchallenged literary canon for four centuries. Even today he is a superb poet and playwright but he is being discarded for his social ideas which are in total contrast, even detrimental to the literature of marginality. Shakespeare's treatment of women characters and the way he presents that great moor Othello makes him sexist and racist. Literature of marginality, thus, opposes the canons of literature. Dalit literature has already refused to be evaluated by the middle-class literary standards, and though it has really yet to establish its own independent standards, it, by and large, has become a discipline demanding an independent enquiry. Dalit poetry which is being produced prolifically, speaks in altogether different semiotics. The image used by dalit poets offers altogether different signs, structure and significance. *Golpeetha*—perhaps the most celebrated collection of dalit poetry—is the most interesting example of new poetry in Marathi. Vijay Tendulkar who wrote Introduction to *Golpeetha* admits his ignorance about certain images used by Dhasal. Vijaya Rajdhyaksha, another important critic in Marathi, is painfully conscious about the languages, the metaphors, the symbols employed by the poet of *Golpeetha*. She is at

Dalit Literature and African-American Literature

a loss to understand the kind of poetry Dhasal writes, and yet she, like, Vijay Tendulkar, is mysteriously drawn towards this poetry. The new poetic diction, a loose carefree yet pleasantly bold poetic structure marks the poems in *Golpeetha*. Here are some examples:

> When Darkness encountered the sun
> words thundered
> How long shall we remain trapped
> Suffocating in the prison-hole of Hell?
> Reborn through free verse
> We shall explode your adulterous myth—said words.
> Hit, O Sakhya, It's your turn now
> If democracy dies let it die.
> Strike at the System itself, O comrade
> A corpse shall not be lighter by removing its pubic hair.

Here is an obvious attempt to subvert the norms of conventional poetry and these attempts to distort the conventional as inevitable as the modernist writer's attempts at technical innovations and experimentation in which language often gets distorted. This is so, particularly in poetry. Poets like Daya Pawar, Waman Nimbalkar, Yashwant Manohar, Keshav Meshram, Tryambak Sapkale—younger poets like Baban Chahande, Lokanath Raipure, Bhau Panchbhai, B. Rangrao, Shiva Ingole, Damodhar More and several others continue to write poetry which challenges the old canons of Marathi literature. Namdeo Dhasal again, particularly his *Golpeetha*, reigns supreme in the realms of Dalit poetry. How anxious he is to subvert the literary norms and throw away the canons is demonstrated here: Plato, Aristotle, Archimedes, Socrates, Marx, King Ashok, Hitler-Bitler, Camus, Kafka, Sartre, Baudelaire, Rembo, Ezra Pound, Hopkins, Goethe, Dante-Bante, Dostoevsky, Mykovasky, Maxim Gorky, Edison-medison, Kalidas, Tukaram, Shakespeare, Dnyaneshwar—who are these all? Let them go down into the gutter mainhole.

The Dalit Poet has learnt to challenge the world canons from the native apathy and indifference. He is open and outright in his revolt against the native tyranny. To quote Namdeo Dhasal again:

> I do not feel respect for you,
> I do not sing of your honour
> I feel like spitting on you the beetle-leaf juice as I hold it in my mouth now
> I want to drown you into potful of semen
> I curse you, curse your scripture, your culture, curse your hypocrisy.

The sort of life the dalits had to face and are still facing is well brought out through the autobiographies. P.E. Kamble's *Aathwaniche Pakshi,* Daya Pawar's *Baluta,* Madhav Kondvilkar's *Mukkam Post Devache Gothane,* Shankarrao Kharat's *Talal Antral* and the autobiographies of women writers like those of Shantabai Kamble, Mallika Dhasal, Shanta Kamble and several others, project together the dehumanizing Dalit life they lead.

Dalit literature not only subverts the old canons but also believes in creating new ones. It seeks to reject those conventions and cultural norms which not only marginalised the dalit voice and the voice of other oppressed communities including women. It attempts to create a new paradigm, a new set of value adding up to the contemporary cultural scenario. The event of dalit literature could be understood as a part of the mass culture which marks the postmodernist phase all over the world. It reveals the collective consciousness of community whose voice had remained suppressed through the annals of history. Therefore, Dalit text always draws on the archetypal pattern exploring the sources of Indian history. It brings out dichotomy which always existed between the 'high' and 'low' cultures and attempts to deconstruct the old cultural narrative which it finds highly biased and partial. It stands for a new ideology which includes all sort of remapping of a social territory which had several lapses before, and needed to be reorganised. Literature of the Dalits represents an alternative culture, refusing to be a subaltern any longer. A dalit text is subversive, but not necessarily intimidating. It relates itself to cultural context and speaks for the revival of sociological approach to literary arts. It opposes the obsessive concern with the formal accomplishment, the linguistic expertise and the modernist tendency to look for the meaning of the text within the text itself. It inaugurates a new era of cultural transformation in the Indian context, and inevitably reaches out to the global phenomenon called postmodernism.

African-American literature projects a similar scenario on the horizon of contemporary world literature. Like India, the United States is also a plural society and like our own society in India, there are several cross-currents operating within the nation. We all know that people from different nations in Europe had come to settle down in America in the 16th century. Though they practised the same religious faith and had similar racial features and appearance, they had brought with them the national identity and ethos which in each case is unique. In this already existing heterogeneity was added the black race with the Negroid features. It was, as it seems now, a mole on a beautiful bright face of raw Virgin land.

I have already commented upon the three major novelists after the Harlem renaissance. I have not dwelt upon the Harlem renaissance because as I have explained, much has been said and written on the famous event. Now, I would like to pass a few comments on the contemporary African American literary scenario. The Negro literature has passed through such subsequent phases as black literature, Afro-American literature and finally to African-American literature. You must have already noticed the term 'African' in the nomenclature. It is to suggest and signify the primacy and priority of the blacks who are from Africa in context of the literary activities. African-American literature today opposes several things in the literature of the white Americans. 'Negro' now is no longer a marginal character but a protagonist who asserts his racial identity. He opposes even the earlier image of himself as portrayed by the Harlem writers—a docile, self-conscious, submissive blackman knocking at the door of god who has always been unkind. Jesus Christ is described as the white devil with blue eyes. If at all there is the god benevolent to the Negro, he must be an incarnation of his own image and personality. Why should he be white with a pair of blue eyes? It is this concept of beauty that has destroyed the lives of many black women. Toni Morrison in her famous novel *The Bluest Eye* (1970) demonstrates this remarkably. Among other characters is a girl called Breedlove, who is driven to madness after being raped by her father and the death of her resulting baby. She finds herself unacceptable everywhere and prays for a pair of blue eyes which is the standard of beauty in the world where she exists. She is ultimately ruined as the destiny she longs for is unattainable. Morrison attacks the black community for being carried away by the Anglo-Saxon standards of beauty, and at the same time, brings out the helplessness which drives them towards self-hatred and self-destruction. The image of the Negro popularised by Jazz orchestra during the 1920s is also unacceptable to the present generation of the blacks which takes pride in being called African-American. Jazz music, as most of you must have known, indulges in extreme primitivism. The singer mostly sings the blues or songs modelled thereon and is carried away by the spiritual longing or by the self-torturing worries—*What did I do / to be so black and blue?* The African-American today rejects the image of himself and strikes the pose of a self-confident, most articulate and among the ablest Americans living today. The image of the black Jazz singer is being ridiculed by August Wilson in his famous play *Ma Rainy's Black Bottom*, a play which ran at Broadway theater for several weeks. Ma Rainy was a famous Jazz singer of the 1920s who made the music form and therein the image of God-fearing, docile Negro universally famous. August Wilson hates this image and makes a scathing attack on those among the blacks who propagate it through arts and literature. He is the representative of the present generation of American-African who see themselves as equal to the whites of any ethnic group in America or elsewhere.

Before I pass on to the works of famous three black sisters, let me mention in brief the names and works of major contemporary African-American novelists. Clarence Majore who wrote *Such was the Season* (1987) and *Emergency Exit* (1979). Ismael Read and Al Young, the duo who edit the famous African journal *Quilt*. Read made himself quite controversial when he attacked the concept of black Feminism propounded and propagated by Gloria Naylor and Alice Walker. The black women writers in an attempt to deviate from the concept of white feminism unconsciously projected the image of black made as brute, violent and angry and who is always submissive to the white master. Alice Walker's *The Color Purple* is the story of a woman who is constantly raped by her stepfather and unable to narrate her shameful experiences to anyone, writes letters addressed to God. The liberation of black woman, asserts Walker, is in the hands of a black woman herself. She depicts the two black women engaged in lesbian acts through which Celie, the protagonist, attains enlightenment. Lesbianism neglects the existence of man. It is not necessarily associated with sexual indulgence between women. It is an emotional reliance on one's own sex rather than on the opposite. But Alice Walker's novel had enraged black men in America, and what resulted is history.

'Black Feminism', in an attempt to glorify the black woman, often unconsciously—I repeat unconsciously—defamed her male counterpart. A passage from *The Bluest Eye* by Toni Morrison makes this point explicit:

> Edging into the life from the backdoor. Becoming. Everybody in the world was in a position to give them order, White woman said—'Do this-, white men said 'come here' Black men said 'lay down'. The only people they need not take order were black children and each other.
>
> But they took of all that and recreated in it their own image. They ran the house of white people, and knew it. When white men beat their men, they cleaned up blood and went home to receive abuses from the victim. They beat their children with one hand and stole for them with the other. The hands that felled trees also cut umbilical cords; the hands that wrung the neck of chickens and butchered hog

also nudged African violets into bloom, the arms that loaded sheaves, bales and sacks rocked babies into sleep. They patted biscuits into flacky ovens of innocence—and shrouded the dead. They ploughed all day and came home to nestle like plume under the limb of their men. The legs that straddled a mule's back were the same one's that straddled their men's hips. And difference was all the differences there was.

In contemporary literature, fiction occupies the most important position, maybe because it catches on the contemporary reality more effectively than any other genre can. While talking of Indian English fiction, Salman Rushdie has called it the only national literature of India. We may not necessarily agree with the basic contention of Rushdie, but the stress he lays on fiction as an important genre today is at least acceptable. In African-American literature, fiction reigns supreme. It is not accident, then, that the Nobel Prize Winner among the contemporary African-American writers is a novelist and a woman for that matter.

In Dalit writing, the place and position of novel as a genre as a literary form unfortunately is not as formidable as African-American novel. Another point of comparison between the two literatures, so to say, is that Dalit Literature refuses to move ahead or at least the discussion on Dalit literary discourse refuses to move ahead. I do not really agree with the view that Dalit literature is stagnated. There are several Dalit youth engaged in writing poems, fiction, short stories etc. What they need is critical encouragement.

Nevertheless, let me state once more that both Dalit literature and African-American literature are no longer literature of marginality. They have become part of mainstream or the mainstream itself in the contemporary postmodern reality.

Some Reflections on Dalit Literature

R.G. JADHAV

Dalit literature signifies a new dimension of the concept of Marginal literature as used in the general literary canon. Dalit literature is typically Indian not only in its roots but also in its purpose and goal. It is addressed to the entire Indian literary tradition and its fulfilment lies in the total transformation of this tradition. Dalit literature is the postcolonial nativistic movement aimed at the cultivation of creative urges of the masses of numerous castes, tribes and communities condemned for centuries to voiceless existence. Dalit literature is the literature of politics and politics is an integral part of it, though politics could be defined in whatever terms one would like to define it. For, Dalitdom is the product of politicisation, a process that is going on continuously in every organised society.

Dalit literature is a collective term in India. Dalit literature is not one, but many. Almost all the major languages and literatures in India have their past and present of Dalit literary expression. Regional linguistic and literary cultures have given peculiar forms to Dalit literatures in India. Numerous Bhakti-cults in different parts of India during the medieval period enabled Dalits to give vent to their suffering and to protest against the tyranny of the unjust socio-religious order. But it is the modern Indian Dalit consciousness that compelled us to discover that lost tradition of medieval Dalit literary battle cry during the post-Independence period. The past is being researched and linked to the aspirations of modern Dalit creativity.

Dalit literature is not only a literature of protest and rejection, but also a literature of reconstruction of the past. Dalit consciousness has inspired intellectuals to probe the entire Indian history and culture from below. This subaltern historical approach has set in motion a process for the true discovery of India. Western orientation is laid to rest and a new image of Bharat is being built up by the scholars inspired by Dalit world-view.

Dalit literature is based on the fundamental human values. It believes that man is the measure of all things including arts, literature and culture. Dalit literature subscribes to secular values like individuality, liberty, equality and fraternity etc. but at the same time does not rule out religion. Religion should provide ethical base to human behaviour in social system. Religion should be a principle and not a law. This approach underlined by Dr. Ambedkar neatly strikes the balance between modern secular values and the individual religious faith.

Dalitness in Indian context is not a monotype reality. It is, in fact, a vast plural concept. Dalit unity in India is full of enormous diversity. Womanfolk in India is a vast Dalit world in itself. All higher and lower castes and classes have held their womenfolk in Dalitdom. Woman in India is a pan-Indian Dalitness. Each caste and tribe here suffers from a peculiar sort of Dalit condemnation. Even the converts to Christianity and Islam are condemned to casteist stigma and taboos. Each caste is sandwiched between a higher caste above and a lower caste below. Thus Dalitness in India is multi-layered and becomes an organic part of all the people belonging to mass society. This sort of multi-faceted grass-root reality of Dalitness in India naturally finds its expression in the post-Independence Dalit literatures in India.

Protest against the established unjust social order and rejection of the entire hegemonic tradition done overtly or covertly, was the main thrust of the modern Dalit literatures in initial stages. But things were changing at a rapid speed and since 1980s, we find internal tensions to which creative minds of Dalits are being subjected. One source of tensions seems to be the ideological conflicts and the second source appears to be the realisation of Dalit cause on the part of non-Dalit sections of the society. Protagonists of Dhamma as propounded by Dr. Ambedkar, the torch-bearers of Ambedkarism, the erstwhile leftists and

Marxists, the right-wing intellectuals and almost all the political parties came forward to appropriate Dalit cause for their own ends, programmes and plans. Dalit literature, Dalit consciousness, Dalit aesthetics, Dalit revolution, Dalit arts etc. all such concepts are thrown in the ideological whirligig. Different ideological views established their own literary canon to admit and to evaluate what constitutes Dalitness in literature. This ideological fervour in post-1980s has certainly affected Dalit literary outputs. From the socio-cultural and aesthetic points of view, this post-80s phenomenon needs to be studied seriously and deeply.

Dalit literature is a new significant identity of modern Indian literature. It is the symbol of distinctive Indian creativity and thus has an easy passage to the corridors of world literature. It is because Dalit literature implies the greatest conflict of human values. This magnificent core must be matched by equally great literary craftsmanship. For this we need men of genius who will successfully ride the wave of ideological tug of war and lead us to the basic human predicament, for which all of us are guilty.

We all must help to prepare this path for the great men of letters to come. For this, sober and balanced critical activity should be intensified and Dalit works analysed in detail and evaluated continuously. Secondly, comparative perspective should be evolved so that Dalit works in one particular Indian language could be compared and estimated in the context of another Indian language. Comparative literature is the need of the hour not only in relation to Dalit literature but Indian literatures as a whole. That will also help us to determine what is Indianness in modern Indian literatures. The critical and comparative studies of medieval Indian literatures will also go a long way to link our past with the present on the basis of Indianness. It will be seen that medieval Indian literatures lead themselves to comparative studies because of their common frame of values based on Bhakti cults while modern Indian literatures provide a common frame of reference which is borrowed from western secular and modern values.

Dalit is a Sanskrit word and means downtrodden, or oppressed or exploited or condemned to peripheral living. These attributes seem to be the eternal attributes of human society. Dalitness is a permanent corresponding reality in human affairs. It is universal and is present in one form or the other in all societies in the world barring the tribal folks. Dalitdom is a parallel humanity, a world in itself subjected to the dynamics of history in terms of continuity and change. Dalit literature in India awakens us to this basic perception of human condition. Dalit reality in India over the long period is an exceptionally unique phenomenon, and if understood properly, should make such perception compulsive for any human mortal.

Attributes of Dalitness go on taking newer forms as the times change, although its core remains the same. Dalits in pre-Independence era were not the same as their medieval predecessors or their post-Independence followers. These changing patterns of Dalitdom naturally find expression in modern Dalit literature in India. Different ideologies emphasize and exploit to their own ends historical claims of Dalitdom and die a natural death with the passing of that particular historical phase. Literature is something that tries to transcend history, the birth and death wedded to historical epochs. Dalit writers of the day surely know this. Their task is to honour the demands of history and at the same time also honour the demands of art and aesthetics. This is obviously a difficult task, but not that impossible.

In conclusion, it may be stated that the concept of Dalit literature constitutes a contribution to aesthetics of literature and opens up an ever-expanding world of Dalitness before creative minds of today and tomorrow. This perception is basically a perception of eternal human sufferings and existentialist predicament. Dalits of today may not remain Dalit tomorrow but their place will be occupied by new Dalits. This perception is tremendously thrilling and has the potentials for building new monuments and mansions of literary creations. Dalit literature as a literature of marginality is thus destined to become a paradigm of world literature wherein marginality breeds profound awareness of undying human spirit struggling with inhuman condemnation of man by man.

Dalit Literature:
A Historical Background

M.D. NALAVADE

Historical background of Dalit writers in India means an account of the rise of Dalit writers in their native land. The terms 'Dalit' and Dalit writers are a new phenomenon in the life, literature and history of India. Dalits as a matter of fact, have no literary history of their own and they had produced no literature till the last quarter of the nineteenth century.

The names, however, like Shambuka in the *Ramayana*, Eklavya in the *Mahabharata*, Valmiki, the great composer and poet of the *Ramayana* and a few others in the ancient times and Chokhamela, Rohidas and some others in the medieval period could be accepted as the great predecessors of the present Dalits. Unfortunately, none of them has left behind any kind of literature which could at least furnish some account of their own and their people.

Hindu literature, one has to admit, is not all-inclusive and deals with life and aspirations of Brahmins. It does not talk about the life and aspirations of the shudras, especially of the downtrodden people, even if they form nearly one-fourth of the Hindu population. Since the dawn of Hindu civilization, the art of writing has been monopolised by the Brahmins and because Brahmins stand on the highest top of Hindu society, they never cared for others in the Hindu society. Naturally, as the untouchables in Hinduism, i.e. present Dalits are supposed to be at the lowest rung, worst of the treatment was given to them by the Brahmins. For ages together, they were not allowed to learn and without acquiring the art of learning it was impossible for them to write about their own life. The Dalits were also the victims of social condition that prevailed in the Hindu society. As a result, in the vast land of India, no Dalit was declared literate until the mid-nineteenth century. No wonder there exists no Dalit literature.

In the Brahminical literature, the kind of treatment meted out to the Dalits seems to be equal to the treatment given to the third rate citizens or to the persons in the enemy nations. Such Brahmins and the so-called literary elites in the past had never allowed their pen to depict the life of Dalits. This has, therefore, made the whole of Hindu literature the literature of the Brahmins. Their literature is not only about the Hindu kings and queens but about the kings and queens of other religions in India. This demands a re-examination because that literature glorifies those who upheld, helped and supported them and criticises those who followed an impartial way. Dalits never appear in their literature on the grounds that Dalits should be treated like that according to the orders and practices of *Manusmriti*. Rightly therefore, D.P. Das[1], a Bengali Dalit, writes in his autobiography that "We do not exist" in the Hindu literature. The Dalit writers therefore have to start from non-existence and from total ban on their learning to beginning of learning and taking education and becoming writers.

The term 'Dalit' has now reached all the corners of India and it has also drawn attention of foreign literary persons and academicians. Unfortunately, in its own native land, it has an abject name and the people recognised as Dalits have still a low status in society. In etymology and in the dictionaries of all Indian languages, it has a derogatory meaning, so also in the literary works of traditional Hindu writers it has no place. As a result, no treatise has been written on the life of Dalits till Dr. Bhimrao Ramji alias Babasaheb Ambedkar started his writings on the tragedies and agonies of Dalits.

Hindu scriptures and social structure prevent the Dalits from receiving education, training and knowledge. The division of the Hindus into two main groups, the Dvija i.e. twice born and the

Advijas or non-dvijas that is, one time-born is man-made and unnatural. Division of the Dvijas into three groups, namely the Brahmins, Kshatriyas, and Vaishyas who are privileged for the right of the Upanayana rite, that is thread ceremony, are supposed to be high caste Hindus wherein brahmins got conferred on themselves the sole right not only to govern the Hindu people but even gods. In Sanskrit, there is an appropriate hymn which describes as to how Brahmins controlled and dominated gods. The hymn runs as follows:

> This universe is possessed by God.
> God is possessed by Mantras.
> The Mantras are possessed by the Brahmins,
> God Himself hence says Brahmins are His Gurus, masters.[2]

Manusmriti therefore asks Hinduism and Hindu kings to maintain and preserve, so also protect 'Dharma' and that 'Dharma' means caste system in which Shudras are not allowed to get education and rise to the status of gaining human dignity and honour. This has therefore created a 'Dark Age' of thousands of years for Dalits in the past even though there was no race other than the upper caste Hindus. As a result of this, ancestors of the Dalits lived the life of unending injustice, torture and heinous treatment. Because of this type of treatment meted out to them, they are compared with the Afro-Americans. This is wrong on the ground that Afro-Americans are racially different; the Dalits are not different from other Hindus or caste Hindus or Brahmins. It is because of this fact and because of the revolution that Dr. Ambedkar brought among the Dalits, they are abused by the upper caste Hindus as Dalit-Brahmins.[3]

On the origin of the caste system, there are a good number of authorities, foreign and native. Their opinions naturally differ from one another. It is a knotty problem, among the scholars, as a correct clue to name thousands of castes and sub-castes of Hindus are not within the reach unless a kind of hypothesis is applied to name the castes. However, the findings of Dr. Ambedkar in this regard are very close to truth. Volumes three and four of his *Writings and Speeches* published by the Government of Maharashtra are a testimony to this fact. What he writes about the degradation of Dalits in the past, helps us to understand their exact position. He states: "rights and disabilities were not based on general uniform considerations. They were based on communal considerations. All rights for the first three varnas and all disabilities for the Shudras was the principle on which the Brahmanic law was based."[4]

Dr. Ambedkar's theory of the origin of Shudras is based on his study of Hindu scriptures. According to him, Shudras have their origin in the Solar race. They are further divided into two groups: the settled community and Broken Men i.e. unsettled community. The Broken Men are those who are debarred from mixing up with the settled community, 'when the cow became sacred and beef eating became a taboo"[5]. And in the course of time the settled community is treated as "touchable" and the Broken Men as untouchables. During all these times, from ancient times this untouchability has been protected and supported by the Hindu rulers as a part of their main function of preserving and protecting Dharma—Hinduism. Muslim rulers also followed the same tradition, though they had to do nothing with the Hindus but they did so merely to please the Brahmins. It was only in the British regime that the royal protection to Hinduism was discontinued and caste system challenged. The social disabilities act of 1850 and the Queen's Proclamation of 1857 threaten the very basis of graded social structure granting inborn honour and facilities more and more to the people in the ascendancy scales and dishonour and disabilities to the people in the descendancy scale. On the one hand, the Queen's Proclamation assures non-interference in the religious matters of the Hindus and on the other hand, it guarantees both the Brahmins and the Non-Brahmins job opportunities on the basis of educational attainments. It has thus made inroads into the protective field of the Brahmin prerogatives. The self-styled intellectual Brahmins yet have not understood the contradiction in the Queen's Proclamation. This facilitated the growth of education and the untouchables got inspiration to learn and stand in the competitive world.

Dalit Writers in Pre-Ambedkar Period

Although the social disabilities removing act of 1850 and the Queen's Proclamation of 1857 stand as landmarks in the educational history of the Dalit; no one among the Brahmins was prepared to teach them. Even the progress in that regard achieved by the Christian missionaries finds comparatively no commendable response. The term naturally then comes of a courageous native named Mahatma Jyotirao Govindra Phule (1827-1890)[6]. He determined to eradicate caste system and establish social equality in the Indian society. Being a Shudra and because of his caste named Mali, which is considered above the untouchables, he also became a victim of casteism. Therefore he opened schools and started teaching those who were prohibited to learn and take education for ages. He also opened special schools, the first one in India for the untouchables of Pune in 1851 A.D. Simultaneously, he worked for the awakening of the masses and social reforms. He is the first among the non-Brahmins in India who started the social reform movement known as the 'Satya Shodhak Samaj' on 23rd September 1873 at Pune. He wrote in the same period a good number of pamphlets and books. His famous books[7] *Gulamgiri*—slavery, *Shetkaryancha Aasud*—Peasant's Whip, *Sarvajanik Satya Dharma*—Universal True Religion, and others bear testimony to the desire of non-Brahmins for reconstructing India on the basis of the classless society. As a writer he is epoch-making because it is he who visualised India as a democratic nation after the British. In understanding and interpreting Hindu scriptures, he stands as a unique visionary and a harbinger of the non-Brahmin and Dalit writers.

Literature is a vast and unlimited field. It is and must be open to all. However, no man can acquire the art of writing unless he has freedom to learn. In India, in all periods except the Buddhist period, the non-Brahmins and the untouchables have been prevented from learning. Hence, because of the want of learning no writers were produced in these periods of history. In the second half of the nineteenth century, during the British regime in India, for the first time non-Brahmins started writing.

Next to Mahatma Phuley stands Krishnarao Bhalekar who started a non-Brahmin newspaper *Deen Bandhu*[8] in 1888 from Mumbai. Many more non-Brahmins and Dalits were inspired by Mahatma Phule. The movement was further strengthened by Shahu Chatrapati[9], the ninth king of the Kolhapur, in Maharashtra. He is the pioneer of the social democracy as Dr. Ambedkar states in one of his letters[10]. The Shahu of Kolhapur started schools and Boarding houses for the non-Brahmins and the Dalits. He also started a movement for asserting the religious rights of the non-Brahmins, which later on converted into the 'Brahmanettar' movement. As a result non-Brahmins and Dalits got inspiration to express their respective viewpoints through their writings.

From the last quarter of the nineteenth century, Dalits started writing and publishing their agonies, hardships and inhuman treatment given to them by the Brahmins and caste Hindus through pamphlets and small booklets. In Maharashtra, Gopalbaba Valangkar,[11] a Mahar by caste and retired Hawaldar from the British Army, wrote and published his first booklet bearing the title *Vital Vidhransak Pustika* in 1888 and some articles about the tragic life of his people in the Marathi weekly *Deen Bandhu*, edited by Narayanrao Lokhande from Mumbai. Gopalbaba criticises the Brahmin suzerainty over the Hindus and holds them responsible for the degradation of his own people and how Brahmins have deceitfully ruined them and grabbed power and prestige. He boldly asked them to understand the Brahmins and stand united to fight against them.

In Maharashtra and in other parts of India, there are some important Dalit writers in pre-Ambedkar period. Pandit Kondiram and Kisan Phagoji Bansod from the central provinces have also attacked the Brahmins through their writing. Gopalbaba Valangkar is the only writer of those days who wrote in English also to organise public opinion against the stoppage of untouchable youths's recruitment into British army. Shivaram Janaba Kamble from Pune has also made sincere intellectual efforts through his writings and social reform activities. His writings[12] are the testimony of his career as a Dalit writer of eminence. But

Dalit Literature: A Historical Background

overall contribution of all those Dalit writers to literature is rather negligible, as it was just the beginning of the Dalit literature.

India is a nation which has many linguistic regional groups and in each of such groups the untouchables have the language of that region and sometimes their own. It is therefore always difficult to study all the languages and find out names of Dalit writers of different regions in India in pre-Ambedkar times. In pre-Ambedkar period, the Dalits remained ununified and no movement either of the literary activity or social reform took place as it did after the rise of Dr. B.R. Ambedkar. Even to Dr. Ambedkar, it was not Marathi, his mother tongue, that helped him; it was through English language that he created a united front and a unifying force for all the Dalits in India. However, it is found from the writings of Dalits in different parts of India, that there is the same voice and expressions of agonies and tragedies under the religious slavery of Hindus. In the erstwhile Hyderabad state of Nizam, next to Bombay Presidency of that time, Dalits had started their social and literary activities in pre-Ambedkar times. Under the leadership of M.V. Bhagya Reddy,[13] Arigay Ramaswamy, M.L. Andiah and others, organisations like the "Jagar Mitra Mandali," "Manya Sanghm" which was later named as the "Adi-Hindu Social Service League of Hyderabad" were found and schools started imparting primary education to the children of Mala community. In the context of India as a whole and the Dalits having their identity of their own as oppressed community in India during that period, no magnetic power or leadership existed to unite them and inspire to write and even to make them fight for their rights.

In the field of social reforms as well as in the literary field, because of the constraints of time and age-old sense of inferiority among the Dalits, no Dalit writer stood on all-India-level to inspire and instruct his brethren to stand erect to seek their legitimate rights in the Indian society. The Dalits, that is, the untouchables still continued the life of slavery under the Hindus. Mr. Das, therefore, writes against this situation as follows: "The Indian untouchables form a thick crust of faceless and nameless human anthill which has no singer of its own agonies. In social arena, it is the high caste Hindu reformers who were for them." (xi)

He further writes that there is a tremendous vacuum in literature in regard to the viewpoint of the underdogs. In Hindu literature, there is formidable tragedy of the pitiable absence of the life of the untouchables. He again states how the untouchables have no rich heritage in the literature as it is in American literature like Paul Dunbar Langston Hughes, Andre Razakarifo; Claude Mackay who wrote in his White House:

> Your door is shut against my tightened face.
> I am sharp as a steel with discontent. (xi)

It is thus, in the pre-Ambedkar period that the movement of Dalit writers faces difficulties in its rise on two grounds. First the bans on their education was lifted in comparatively the recent past and secondly, on all India level they have no common language of their own. Even though some efforts were made by some writers, they did not grow as a live wire in the literary field. However, it is to be admitted that in the caste ridden and Brahmin dominated Hindu society, the efforts of known and unknown Dalit writers in pre-Ambedkar period have primarily done yeomen's service to express the aspirations of their awakened brethren.

Dr. Ambedkar: Father and Doyen of Dalit Literature

Dalit Literature in pre-Ambedkar times and after the rise of Dr. Ambedkar marks a clear-cut two different identities. In the first place, even if there is an urge to free Dalits from the Hindu slavery and ask Dalits to give up traditional way of life and in the second place to inspire the Dalits to acquire the art of writing. All that Dr. Ambedkar wanted to achieve through his social and literary activities was to make Dalits assert their position as human beings. In his speech at the Mahad Satyagraha, he says: "We are not going to Charadav Lake merely to drink its water.

We are going to the lake to assert that we too are human beings like others."[14]

The rise and life-time of Dr. Ambedkar is the real foundation period of the all-round rise and growth of Dalits in India. It has multi-marvellous facets which adorn the careers of present Dalit writers who are more fortunate because Dr. B.R. Ambedkar has to his credit a very rich and unprecedented golden heritage of writings on varied subjects and more particularly on the ancient and Sanatan Hindu scriptures. He has very ably brought to the forefront drawbacks and contradictions in the Hindu scriptures and literature. Simultaneously, he has evolved his own theories to establish a new philosophy and even to create an atmosphere for counter attacks.[15] The message of all his writings is to create a humane atmosphere in India and to consolidate various social forces which the Brahminic rule had created in the name of Hinduism. Similarly, to emancipate the downtrodden to play their roles in the national life of India is the most important message, for unity and integrity. His wish to create India as a great nation through social and economic revolution without bloodshed as the real democratic state is the everlasting gift to the people of India. His writings and speeches, published by the government of Maharashtra is more than enough to know his enormous intellectual ability and wisdom par excellence. In fact, his place in Indian literature is unique and uncompromising as a doyen. Rightly, therefore, all the literary movements of Dalits, as well as all Dalit writers proudly hold him in high esteem as the father of Dalit literature.[16]

Dr. Ambedkar's role in piloting the drafting of the Constitution of India and getting the highest unprecedented honour as the chief architect of the Constitution, is unique and most revered. It asks the Dalit writers to rise above all in the intellectual pursuits and literature. His famous books, *The Buddha and His Dhamma, Who were the Shudras, Annihilation of Caste, The Problem of Rupee in British India, Thoughts on Pakistan* and others which have been published by the Government of Maharashtra in seventeen volumes, stand as the cut-off line in the past and beginning of new epoch in the cosmopolitan living and writings of

Independent India. Dalit writers have this ideal before them, their destination is not undecided but is carried out in the form of Dr. Ambedkar's spirit of patriotism and nationalism. It is against the spirit and message of Dr. Ambedkar that they are striving to stand as writers in the literary world.

Dalit Writers and Literary Movements

Dr. Ambedkar is the apostle of the Dalits. Historically again, he is the first to break Sanatan Hindu traditions of ban on learning for the untouchables. His own achievements in the field of learning are the source of pride, prestige and inspiration to the Dalits. Because, first, Dalits were supposed to be ineligible to learn due to want of blessings from Goddess of learning and secondly, no man among the Dalits has risen previously to the height of Dr. Ambedkar at the caste level, as well as on the national level. Thus, none else but Dr. Ambedkar alone stands as an ideal, for the people of the downtrodden castes. Bhimrao Kardak born in 1904 in the Nasik District was a poet, balladeer and a writer in his own humble way. He tells how he was thrilled to attend, for the first time in his life, the public meeting of Dr. Ambedkar, the Bar-at-law.

In a poem written in 1931, Kardak as a balladist holds Dr. Ambedkar as God and appeals in humility to bestow upon himself poetic ability and intellect that will be required to describe Dr. Ambedkar completely. He also says that Dr. Ambedkar is born to emancipate them i.e. the Dalits.

In the present circumstances, young literates and foreigners will not understand correctly as to why earlier Dalit writers, poets and other people held Dr. Ambedkar as their messiah, or emancipator. In the land of gods and temples, Dalits have seen through ages together, that no god, no incarnation had freed them to live as others do. Rightly therefore, Dr. Ambedkar is more revered and he is very dear to the Dalit heart. Naturally, most Dalit writers in early phase have expressed their humble gratitude in their writings, for Dr. Ambedkar's unprecedented role in their upliftment, progress and emancipation. The rise of such writers comes under the first phase according to B.S. Hate and it starts from the Mahad Satyagraha of 1927 and Jalasakar K.K. Salri, Valangkar, Bhimrao Kardak, L.G. Salave-Vahurkar, C.B. Khairmode and others are the pioneers of Dalit writings.

In the second phase, the number of Dalit writers seems to have increased. But their writings are considered to be not in tune with the Hindu tradition and found no chances of publication till Dr. Ambedkar started his weekly paper *Janata* in 1930. Then a group of Dalit writers were attracted and fascinated towards community ideology as their economic needs were to be chartered by the communists. However, most Dalit writers seemed disgusted to see their writings wrapped into red colour and returned to their homes. Thus even if historically it is correct to see different stages of Dalit writers, all the writings that they have during all such stages have very much common themes. And in general, these themes could be divided into five categories, as under:

1. Against social disabilities forced upon Dalits.
2. Hindu caste system and inhuman treatment to Dalits
3. Dr. Ambedkar's demand of social equality
4. Dr. Ambedkar's stand for social justice.
5. Buddhism and social and economic democracy

The themes chosen by Dalit writers are the natural outcome of their expressions. In the short stories, poems, ballads, novels, biographies, autobiographies, dramas, historical writings and all other forms of literature, they have created their own sphere of influence. Educationally, the qualifications of all such writers vary from formal education of fourth standard to Ph.D. degrees. Their standings in society also vary from ordinary farm labours, textile mill workers, teachers professors , to university Vice-Chancellors and I.A.S. officers and advocates. Naturally, no theme of their social interests and interests of their community remains untouched by them. All these themes, their experiences, and viewpoints are unknown to literature, written by Brahmins and upper caste Hindus. This certainly created a new world of experience in the Indian literature.

Mr. Shankarrao Kharat who has received unique honour of presiding over all India Marathi Sahitya Sammelan—the annual gathering of all the Marathi writers—one of the most revered and recognised honour in the literary field, is a Dalit and a staunch follower of Dr. Ambedkar. His autobiography *Taral Antaral* is read in all circles of society. It gives accounts of Dalit life, particularly of Mahars in Maharashtra. Professor Angane Lal from Lucknow was also a Vice-Chancellor like Shankarrao Kharat and has to his credit, books on philosophy and historical writings. Mr. Bhagwan Das from Delhi, L.R. Bag from Jallandhar, Dr. Munshilal Gautam from Aligarh, Keshav Meshram and Vaman Hoval from Mumbai, Yashwant Manohar from Nagpur, Dr. Gangadhar Pantawane from Aurangabad, Geeta Nagbhushan from Karnataka, Namdeo Dhasal, Raosaheb Kasabe, Vasant Rajas, Professor Parameshwar from Hyderabad, Dr. Jamanadas Khobragade from Chandrapur and many more, in hundreds, have a name on the literary horizon as Dalit writers and as creating a new saga by way of their writings.

Mr. Shankarrao Kharat who has very ably but prudently depicted in his *Taral Antaral* the tragic life of Mahars in the outskirts of villages and writes that in those days no schools were available to the children of Mahars and Mangs (65) when he was at the age of going to school. He also describes how in his boyhood people of Mahar community used to speak proudly of Dr. Babasaheb Ambedkar, his incomparable and unprecedented achievements in studying abroad and how they held him wiser and cleverer than the Brahmins and determined to follow him alone. (247)

Dalit writers thus have created their own image in all the Indian languages including Urdu. In all parts and corners there are Dalit writers and through their writings and literary movements they have now captured the whole of holy lands of India to imprint their letters of their agonies in the past and dreams of future. They all are hypnotised by the message, preachings and teachings of Dr. Ambedkar. They have now acquired the art of writing through which they are determined to free their brethren from the Dark Age, that Brahmins and Hinduism created for them in the past and stand along with their brethren to look forward to the world of knowledge and prosperity. All Dalit writers in all parts of India including Anna Bhau Sathe[17] say in one tone, "strike with might to change the world." Shankarananda Shastri Dr. Sukhdeo Thorat. Geeta Nagbhusan, D.P. Das and hundreds of other Dalit writers in various parts of India have now earned status as established writers. And what they wish for their people and for India as a whole could well be mentioned in the words of D.S. Das: "To the fundamentalist proponents of Hindu way of life I would like to offer a word of counsel. Since I belong to untouchable fraternity, they may be inclined to suspect my motive. In spite of this danger, I should not flinch from my duty. India they seem to visualize cannot be very strong and vibrating country unless they totally reform and regroup discarding the huge monolith named, Varnasram.[18] And in the limited objectives, Dalit writers speak the tongue of Bandhumadhav as he writes: "Just as the Russian writers helped the revolution by spreading Lenin's revolutionary ideas . . . our writers should spread Dr. Ambedkar's philosophy to the villages."[19]

After all, the Dalit writers follow the message of Dr. Babasaheb Ambedkar and their literature has man at its centre. And as Dr. M.N. Wankhade states: "The pens of the Dalit writers are ready as levers, to lift the people's democracy out of the mud of anarchy."[20] It is thus Dr. Ambedkar's message and teaching work which is the magnetic force in the background of Dalit writers.

NOTES

1. D.P. Das, *The Untouchable Story* (New Delhi: Allied, 1985), Introduction, p. xii.
2. Sanskrit Shlok, Devadhin Jagat.
3. Daya Pawar, *Balutan* (An autobiography) (Mumbai: Granthali, sixth ed., 1995), p. 1.

4. Dr. Babasaheb Ambedkar, *Writings and Speeches* (Mumbai: Govt. of Maharashtra, 1990), Vol. 7, *Who were the Shudras*, p. 61.
5. Ibid., *Untouchable*, p. 370.
6. Keer Dhananjay, *Mahatma Jyotiba Phule* (Mumbai: Popular Prakashan, 1964), p. 3.
7. M.P. Mangudkar, *Mahatma Phule and Satyashodhak Chalwal* (Pune: Social Book Stall, 1954), pp. 61-62.
8. Keer Dhananjay, *Mahatma Jyotiba Phule*, pp. 146-47.
9. Keer Dhananjay, *Shahu Chatrapati* (Mumbai: Popular Prakashan, 1976), p. 203.
10. M.D. Nalawade, ed., *Lokshahi Dandak Weekly* (Kolhapur).
11. Gopalbaba Valangkar belonged to Ravdhal village in Konkan region of Maharashtra. After his retirement as a Hawaldar from the British Army in 1886, he worked as an associate of Mahatma Phule and also started an independent organisation for the upliftment of his people. The organisation Anarya Dosha Pariharak Mandali was also established by him in 1893.
12. H.N. Nawalkar, *Shivram Kamble*, Sugawa Prakashan, Pune 30, reprinted in 1997.
13. M.V. Bhagya Reddy, a Mala by caste had adopted his name from the original Madari Bhagiah. Hence there was lot of controversy between him and the real Reddy. See for other names and details, P.R. Venkatswamy, *Our Struggle for Examination*, Vol. I (Hyderabad, 1955), pp. 3-13.
14. Arjun Dangle, ed., *Poisoned Bread* (Translation from Modern Marathi Dalit Literature) (Mumbai: Orient Longman, 1992) (Dr. Ambedkar's Speech at Mahad), p. 225.
15. Dr. Babasaheb Ambedkar, *Writings and Speeches* (Mumbai: Govt. of Maharashtra Publication, 1987), Vol. 3, pp. 416-37.
16. Dangle, p. 237.
17. Bajrang Korde, *Anna Bhau Sathe—Makers of Indian Literature* (New Delhi: Sahitya Akademi, 1999), p. 73.
18. Das, Introduction, p. xv.
19. Dangle, p. 242.
20. Ibid, p. 319.

Dalit Literature: A Minority Discourse

V.D. PHADKE

I need to introduce two caveats at the very beginning of this article: that is a bird's eye view of the Dalit literature, and that it is more about the socio-cultural politics around Dalit literature rather than Dalit literature itself or its criticism. It must also be clarified here that Dalit literature includes the literature by the Dalit writers originally in Marathi and whatever little of that is translated in English. The term 'Dalit' here includes all those who were earlier called untouchables; all except those belonging to the three so-called 'upper' castes.

Rhetoricians may say that it is not a good strategy to begin a written composition with caveats. But logicians may be glad to note that the matrix of the composition is clear to the writer. This clarity must be directed firstly to the mischief played by the dominant culture in calling Dalit literature a minority discourse. It must be exposed that a minority has been masquerading as the majority and suppressing the demographic majority. This perversion is a hallmark of the caste system. By a rough estimate, the 'mainstream' consisting of the so-called 'high' castes means three-and-half per cent of the population only! It is almost a socio-political miracle that the culture of ninety-six and half per cent has been condemned as peripheral, marginal and minor—that too for generations.

The dominant culture had reserved for itself the exclusive right to read and write. Hence it could express itself through oral as well as written texts. All others, except the three upper castes, viz. the Brahmins, the Kshatriyas and the Vaishyas, were forbidden to read and write. A Shudra found to be listening to the Vedas was to be punished by pouring molten lead in his ears!

Thus deprived of all access to knowledge, and opportunity to contribute to it, the Dalits were condemned to silence, a will-not-be heard predicament. Their share in all aspects of societal life was reduced to a 'minority' status and was ruthlessly maintained that way for ages.

The Indian renaissance in the second half of the 19th century was a result of the attack of aggressive Western imperialism. For the Dalits, this renaissance was carried forward in the 20th century by the messianic figure of Dr. Babasaheb Ambedkar. After his demise in 1956, the organisation supposed to continue his work, i.e. the Republican Party of India, disintegrated. The Dalit movement experienced a short resurgence in the days of the Dalit Panther. The same resurgence also caused the blossoming of Dalit literature in Marathi with sufferance and revolt as the main planks. After the Dalit Panther suffered the same fate as that of the Republican Party, it was only the agitation caused by and for the implementation of the Mandal Commission report that brought the whole question of the 'minorities' to the forefront.

The Dalit sensibility is closely interlinked with the ups and downs in the Dalit struggle. This sensibility manifested itself mainly through poetry and autobiographical fiction. The demands that the dramatic form makes on the playwright have not been met by the Dalit writers convincingly so as to give Dalit drama a prominent place. (This is one area the Dalit thinkers have to ponder over.) If poetry and autobiography have been popular with the Dalit writers because they can accommodate their inevitably torrential emotionalism and if dramatic form is not so popular because of its demands for greater control by the playwright on himself, Dalit literature will certainly have to break the destructive paradox of self-concentration. This means that the formalist approach will not be able to do justice to the achievements of Dalit literature. However, warning bell should be sounded against strict adherence to the socio-politico-anthropological criteria as the only acceptable approach of literary criticism of Dalit literature.

In the heydays of the Dalit Panther, the Dalits were perceived as a monolith. It was not so in the 1980s. The readers of Dalit literature became aware that there are numerous particularities within them. More disturbing was the awareness that there is a hierarchy within Dalits, within the last lowest rung of the caste system, ladder. One obvious example is that of Dalit women. Others, like Dr. Kishore Shantabai Kale, were out of the caste system because they were not legally recognised as legitimate children. Their autobiographies, in a way, deconstructed the very authenticity of revolt in Dalit literature. The tribals were the most marginalised and articulated their protest against the 'upper' castes as well as the 'respectabilised' Dalits.

Even though its essence was negation Dalit literature could not wash off either the idiom or the modes and forms of the middle class, 'Sadashivpethi'[2] established canon of the 'mainstream' Marathi literature. Critics like Dr. Sudhir Rasal have observed that the language of Dalit literature remained respectable Marathi. The imagery of Dalit poetry also remained sanskritised, with the notable respectable Marathi. The imagery of Dalit poetry also remained sanskritised, with the notable exception of Namdeo Dhasal.

The question of evolving an idiom of their own is important for Dalit literature in more ways than one. Laxman Gaikwad's *Uchalya* begins in the dialect of his community. However, it increasingly shifts to the 'mainstream' Marathi. Is this because of an awareness of the readership which was from the 'enemy' camp? Only 'they' could read and afford to buy books. Hence, the shift in the register? Idiom, as in Shaw's *Pygmalion*, represents the state in which the individual is at the time of usage.

However, Najubai Gavit does not shift to the respectable Marathi in her autobiographical narration. She sticks to her own dialect. Does it mean that the 'respectable' Marathi is (or will be) a stigma? Does it mean that negation of Sadashivpethi establishment is complete? Does this mean a beginning of separation? The answers, the future will yield, will be worth watching.

The term 'postcoloniality' is taken to mean the end of the age of imperialism-colonialism, of exploitation of colonies in Asia and Africa by the Europeans. However, with respect to Dalit literature, it has altogether different connotation. It means the replacement of the external coloniser by the internal coloniser. All the natives were the 'subjects' for the Europeans as they were the external colonisers. During their rule, the Dalits experienced a double colonisation. With the Indian Independence, it gave way only to an internal colonialism. The victims of this internal colonialism, and consequently Dalit literature, have shown a curious affinity towards the external coloniser. Enemy of the enemy should be our friend. It is only because of the onslaught of the external colonisers that the insolence of the internal colonisers was somewhat curbed. It is noteworthy in this context that the foreign aggressions on the Hindu society were greatly responded to by the Dalits with conversions to Christianity and Islam. Hence, there are traces of welcoming tones to the external colonisers.

Contrarily, Dalit literature also displays a commitment to ethnicity. In fact, ethnic in the Indian context may come to mean Dalit, if and when the internal colonisers will assimilate the norms of neo-colonialism. That will be a postcolonial time for Dalit literature. As of now, Dalit literature has yet a long way to go.

That's how Dalit literature stands on the threshold of the twenty-first century. Its canon-formation is not yet comprehensive enough. Dalit literature has served mainly as an instrument of catharsis for the Dalits. They have yet to use the politics of difference constructively. Will it be able to do so in the age of globalisation? Perhaps neo-capitalism may dismantle the caste hierarchy. Or new castes may arise and with them, new ways of internal colonisation. In that case, Dalit literature will have to reformulate itself completely.

DALIT POETRY

L.S. DESHPANDE

There came a stream of writing in Marathi called Dalit Literature in the late 1960s. Its beginning runs parallel to the emergence of the Little Magazines Movement in Marathi—"The angry young man" syndrome and existential philosophy being their common ground. It shares its identity and some of its agony and suffering, too, with Black literature also. Exploitation, more cultural than social or economic, is manifest in every page of it. It is an untold story of the people that have always remained in the dark—unseen, unheard and unsung—with a burden of 5000 years' history on their backs.

Dalit Literature lingered on the periphery of Marathi Literature in the 1970s but began to occupy its due place in the 1980s and is being recognized as almost pivotal to the mainstream of contemporary Marathi literature in the 1990s. But whether one likes it or not, Baburao Bagul, the pioneer of the Dalit short stories, views the established literature of India as "Hindu Literature" and, therefore, expects Dalit Literature to be considered "in the tradition of the great literature of the world."[1]

Dalit literature is seen, in the main, as protest against the establishment as commitment to inculcating new values aiming at a new order. There are in it a lot of frustration, a lot of anger, and a lot of hope, too. It breathes freedom. The protagonist, be it of a poem or a short story, is usually projected as a rebel "standing up against subjugation, humiliation, and atrocities" and is also shown, at times, as "singing intoxicatedly of the dawn of a new life."[2]

The poets are, of course, in the vanguard of Dalit writing. Poetry comes first, followed by other kinds of writing such as autobiography, drama criticism, etc. It is not just modern, but a new kind of writing in terms of experience and sensibility, structure and style. The most notable among the Dalit poets are Narayan Surve, Namdeo Dhasal, Keshav Meshram, Yashwant Manohar, Raja Dhale, Arjun Dangle, J.V. Pawar, Waman Nimbalkar, Tryambak Sapkale, Arun Kamble, Prakash Jadhav, Bhagwan Sawai, Chokha Kamble, etc. among men and Mina Gajbhiye, Hira Bansode, Jyoti Lanjewar, Mallika Amar Sheikh, Anuradha Gurav, Pradnya Lokhande etc. among women.

A Dalit poem is unique in the sense that it builds its structural pattern out of Dalit sensibility. It is unusual, exceptional in terms of experience and expression—something alien to the so-called Marathi middle-class sensibility. It transfers the themes of isolation, alienation, protest, revolt, struggle for survival, freedom from all sorts of bondage and exploitation, apathy, estrangement and uprootedness, a search for new identity, and a longing for human dignity. It is thus a poetry of protest, voicing its opposition to all that is orthodox, traditional and conventional. It is as much empathetic as evocative and addresses itself anew to its reader in terms of startling images and symbols, differently moulded myths and metaphors.

"Priority of life"[3] over everything else in life is what Keshav Meshram claims as a criterion to determine the raison d'être of Dalit literature. For example, these lines from his poem titled 'Addressing God, on a Day' in which the poet is seen heaping abuses after abuses on God, at times in the name of His mother, thus:

> Son of bitch! For a scrap of bread,
> Will you cut up a cart-load of fire-wood?
> Will you wipe sweat off your emaciated body?
> To see father smoke,
> Will you accept straining
> Your brother's your sister's muscles?
> For a gulp of his drink

Will you go pimping? (16, My translation)

God will not do it, the poet knows it for certain, but a mother—so toiling and loving will, by force, do it. It is with these words, at once ironic and compassionate, that the poem ends. The ending of a Dalit poem is often found remarkable in that it gives a kind of jerk that corrects the reader's sensibility, in an unusual manner, restoring it a balance. The unfamiliar is made familiar; familiarization, as opposed to defamiliarization, is a poetic process through which a Dalit poem passes.

Mother-image as a spirit of supreme sacrifice characterizes most of the Dalit writing. The truth of the observation can be witnessed again, in another poem titled 'Money Order'[4] by Narayan Surve, an outstanding poet in the galaxy of the contemporary Marathi poets. The poem takes the shape of a message dictated to the writer at the post office by an illiterate village woman now living in a metropolis. It is written on the coupon of the money order form and is addressed to her kids saying that they will buy with the money their needs, a frock for one, a shirt and a trouser for another, and finally jilebi for all as a part of festivity. In a concluding note, she reminds them not to forget buying their father a new turban for the one he was wearing at the time she left was reduced to tatters. The money she is sending has been earned by "the sweat of her brow," an honest labour's fruit, through forced harlotry in the face of gnawing unemployment. Physically, she is removed from them; but mentally, rather emotionally, she is with them, among them. A careful, loving mother to her kids, a devoted, constant wife to her husband—that is what she is. Sincere and faithful, and more importantly, committed to them all as a member of the family. The poem thus offers a revelation of and an insight into what we refer to as 'new morality' in these days.

One can see the same mother-image in Waman Nimbalkar's 'Mother'[5] and Jyoti Lanjewar's 'Mother'[6], but with a variation on theme and in perspective, viz. the one treats a personal, private experience in a conventional manner and the other has a social dimension to it, projecting a new awakened consciousness.

A Dalit poem may therefore, be seen as a product of this new consciousness. It presages a new caste system, overthrowing the dominance of the so-called middle-class conventional norms and standards. It breaks new grounds in terms of experience, sensibility and expression. It is revolutionary in terms of idiom, diction and style, controverting the established aesthetic norms and literary criteria in Marathi. For example, if there is a choice between truthfulness and elegance, a Dalit writer chooses to be truthful rather than elegant, and that, too, sometimes at the cost of decency. The Dalit writers, particularly the poets, have, to put it in the words of K. Satchidanandan, "created an alternative poetics that throws overboard classical values like propriety, balance, restraint and understatement. They also often use a deliberately subversive diction that challenges middle-class notions of decency."[7]

In his introduction to Dhasal's anthology, *Golpitha,* Vijay Tendulkar remarks: "The Marathi language so softly and delicately nurtured by the white-collared class, so rich in its splendour, Namdeo turns and twists "like a mistress." He shatters it to pieces: he fills it, adding indecent expressions, with deliberate distortions. He justifies it as being warranted by the semantic content of his poem."[8]

Take, for example, his poem 'Hunger'[9]; even in its translated version by Shanta Gokhale, the poem may be seen as a piece of orchestration, for the meaning is born out of its musical pattern. Its theme is: only those who have experienced such self-consuming, other-inflicted hunger know what it means, how painful and incapacitating the state is, something beyond the reach of the middle-class sensibility. Hunger is seen here as a multiple poetic reality and the poet toys with it on physical, mental and emotional levels. Namdeo makes us visualise "the gold-threaded struggle/between the snail of pain/and the sea" and then becomes, all of a sudden, self-introspective, as in the following rhetorical question.

If we have not made ourselves a tidy life,
What right do we have to quarrel with flowers?

See how poetically the poet apostrophises in positive terms, entreating upon it to "say yes to our dreams" and not to "snuff out the orphan huts upon the shore." Hunger on physical level is an awesome, hateful calamity bringing in its wake emotional devastation, but the poet keeps his attitude towards it deliberately frivolous despite all seriousness, e.g.

> Here's our manhood before you now
> Let's see who wins this round
> You are we?

but, then, manages to come out in his own real self, saying, most outspokenly, in abusive terms:

> Then we will screw
> Seventeen generation of you
> Hunger, you and your mother.

The phenomenon of hunger is, thus, first presented in realistic terms and then carried further on into the world of fantasy and, finally, brought back to our workaday world of reality poetising all this in terms of images, similes and metaphors.

A Dalit work is born out of a social situation, out of a social context. It is an outcome as much of social compulsions as of individual creative urges. It is a social document in the sense that it is an imaginative reconstruction of vital truths about their individual lives but as inalienable members of their respective community/ communities. Thus, it is societal rather than individual in character. It sustains itself on liberal, rationalistic, humanitarian ideology mainly drawn from such sources as Dr. Amebdkar's and Mahatma Phule's writings, Marxism and Buddhism. The stunning, heart-rending, traumatic experiences it treats shake the reader's consciousness, destroy his fake sense of self-assurance and self-complacency and finally bring him out of his ivory-tower existence. It wounds his pride by giving expression to its author's fury and frustration but heals the injuries inflicted on him by presenting a vision in which all-encompassing love and compassion are 'cathartic'.

In the light of the foregoing discussion, one may read Bhagwan Sawai's poem 'Tathagata' 'Two Poems'[10]. It is deeply inspired by a process of conversion. The change of creed results, in its final analysis, into a shifting of consciousness from one state to another. The theme emerges from the primordial man's divided mind: of the two highly individualized personal responses of the poet, the first one is orthodox and conventional, whereas the second one is bold and new, and in keeping with the genuine Buddhist faith.

In the first of the twin poems, the primordial man, who is none other than the poet's alter ego, entreats upon Tathagata to ask him no question for two reasons: (i) "questions" are alien to his nature and (ii) "there was nothing but darkness and rocky muteness" in his consciousness. The poet, then, prays to Tathagata to emerge from the portrait and "transmigrate" into his "effusive being." Thus the Hindu consciousness comes in the way of his implanting the new-found creed.

In the second, the same primordial man is seen weeping bitterly at the sight of "The tattered sails of his own floating ship/in the eyes of Tathagata." Then comes a paradoxical couplet, followed by three lines in which the poet is seen giving a vent to mystic realization of his own self using such poetic symbols as "shore," "ocean," and "waves":

> Do not leave me shoreless
> Do not leave me on the shores
> Because
> This ocean is dear to me
> My life-blood mingled in every wave.

The poet, then, regrets his misdemeanour in "worshipping" the image of Tathagata with his "offerings of flowers and prayers" and seeks Tathagata's forgiveness for his blind, foppish act of "fetishism," so inconsonant with the tenets of Buddhism.

Persecution is naturally a very common theme of most Dalit poetry, e.g. "That Single Arm,"[11] by Tryambak Sapkale or "Broken Men"[12] by Daya Pawar. The first poem narrates a fanciful and yet dramatic situation; it is a word picture in which the poet's son is seen as cutting out "the attacker's arm" from his shoulder, of course, in the picture story. The offender's "sliced off" arm shows now as dangling even in its uplifted posture, alarming the world that the days of man's persecution by man are numbered. Similarly, the other poem by Daya Pawar deals with Worli Riots, using as its central image a maimed soldier from the Mahar Batallion who wonders why he was crippled for the country that attacks his people.

A poem more important than these two in the context of persecution, especially of cultural sort, as a shared theme is "Every Harvest, Here"[13] by Namdeo Dhasal. In its English version, the poem may read like this:

> Here every harvest is undone
> No matter, therefore, if you hang
> A bare skeleton on a branch
> Here, no eyeballs reduce the grass splinters
> No matter, therefore, if you break goblets
> Here, no fire burns within
> And all creative urge lies charred
> Here, every great poet looks dwarfish
> So unbecoming it is
> Being allured by felicitous words
> Here, a man eats up a man
> And, eh, the whiplashes on Walya's back stay hidden.
> (My translation)

Love for India is another common theme of a number of Dalit poems; it is perceptible, directly or obliquely, in the doubts or reservations in the course of poem. A sense of belonging is what pervades most of the poems under reference here. One may read, for example, Keshav Meshram's poem titled 'In Our Colony'[14] which puts a question how their houses stand in the outskirt of a village. The answer is "like foot-prints of cattle in the mud." In her poem 'Caves'[15] Jyoti Lanjewar questions the relationship between the land and the people. She is seen asking "How did we get to this place/this land which was never mother to us." Similarly, Uttam Kolgaonkar, too, is straightforward in his poem 'House'[16] narrating the precarious condition of his house in the slums; he says:

> He was born here,
> but didn't belong here

The house looks puny among the skyscrapers: it stands dilapidated, with the rear wall collapsed. The poet says:

> the whole sky
> with its thousand eyes
> had invaded the house.

Moving away from the immediate, local context to the distant, global context, Bapurao Jagtap, in his poem 'This Country is Broken',[17] addresses his brethren, in a tone of pain and anguish mixed with sarcasm, asking them to abandon this land and settle elsewhere.

> where, while you live, you will have
> a roof above your head,
> and where, when you die, there will at least be
> a cemetery to receive you.

This demand for a new land is symbolically speaking, a demand for new people meaning thereby "a new ethos." In his poem titled 'I belong to it'[18] what Arjun Dangle is seeking is a name for his people, for his country,

> whose meaning
> may engrave itself upon my heart,
> and gently blow upon my endless pain.
> It will belong to me and I belong to it.

Dalit Poetry

But the social situation is so devastating that even such a great celebrity among the Dalit writers as Baburao Bagul goes to the extent of propagating violence, for he says:

> You who have made the mistake of being
> Born in this country
> Must now rectify it: either leave the country
> Or make war![19]

Of late there are a number of Dalit women poets, who have contributed to Dalit poetry, in general, and feminist writing in particular.

Among the Dalit women poets, we have Mina Gajbhiye placing "battle" over "song" and that, too, paradoxically enough, in her very first poem publicly recited at the Asmitadarsh Literary Conference in Nagpur in 1976. She says:

> In a song full of hope in the evening
> There's no meaning.
> This is a time to breathe battle.[20]

In her poem titled 'Peace'[21] she is seen saying:

> The crows feeding on funeral feasts cry:
> "the revolution has come
> the revolution has come,"

The cuckoo in their nest is shot dead, singing "her song of pain" "the revolution" goes elsewhere, carrying the cuckoo's song along. Then, the sparrow "fluttering in a pool of blood," leaving the female cry bitterly. The female sparrow comes to his help offering him shade from the sun. There is a storm, along with thundering and lightening in the sky. To the gunman's question wherever she belongs to the party of "Revolution" or to that of "Peace," she replies: "I don't know about that". Presuming that she belongs to the party of "Peace," the gunman pulls the trigger. The poem ends with this couplet:

> Now the female sparrow

goes around searching for peace.

In the teeth of Hindu opposition, Mina Gajbhiye, in her poem "Bodhi Tree"[22] (titled "Pimpalvruksh" in Marathi) seeks to sow the seeds, but, in an anxiety-ridden state, says:

> I am doubtful,
> Will at least one seed sprout?
> Bodhi tree.

Her poem 'The Weeping Wound of Centuries'[23] was written in the aftermath of the massive riots in 1978 for renaming the Marathwada University after Dr. Babasaheb Ambedkar's name. The bonds are snapped, the stitches are ripped open and "the weeping wound of centuries" stands exposed. That makes a lot of difference to the poetess, for she says tellingly:

> From now on I won't scream "I want to live."
> From now I'll live to die.

The ambiguity in the concluding line of the poem is the most impressive; it goes thus:

> I will not live like a pariah dog, nowhere.

Subversion of the established history and myth characterizes most of the Dalit writings; for example, see now Hira Bansode in her famous poem 'Yashodhara'[24] a masterpiece, compares "the darling of her heart" Yashodhara to "a dream of sharp pain, life-long sorrow." Guilt-ridden as she is, she is seen acquiescing: "I don't have the audacity to look to you." And the contrast below between "we" and "you" followed by "brightened" and "absorbs" and yet further by "light" and "dark," respectively in the lines,

> We were brightened by Buddha's light.
> but you absorbed the dark.

Dalit Poetry

The poem moves on, leading from one line to another, and, in the process, flashes this image or that, e.g., the "tender sky" is what comes to Yashodhara "for refuge" or, again, "what pained stars shed tears" at her grief and solitariness. The poetess is moved to tears at the sight of Yashodhara's "matchless beauty" "dimming like twilight" at her estrangement from her loving husband Gautama. Then comes the final master-stroke, with a feminine slant, when she says reassuredly:

> Listening to your silent sighs
> I feel the promise of heavenly happiness.

The poem's success consists in the externalization of its author's mind and consciousness. The dramatic sweep carries the poem through and achieves its marvellous effects. Yashodhara, while her life is slipping by, remembers:

> that last kiss of Siddhartha's final farewell,
> those tender lips.

And the pithy line that follows dwells on Siddhartha's achievement:

> He went, he conquered, he shone.

Juxtaposed with the songs of Buddha's triumph are Yashodhara's femininity, her tearful eyes, and her helplessness. The poetess feels sad and is further stunned at history's silence about the great story of Yashodhara's sacrifice. Neither an epic nor a purana nor even a single Buddhist vihara could accord her a place as if she did not deserve to be reckoned at all. The poetess's heart is filled with shame at all this. However, in the concluding lines of the poem, she is seen giving a twist to the very idea on which she has built her poetic mosaic. She feels reassured and happy at the glimpse of Yashodhara's "beautiful face" which is fondly found hidden no where else than in the small space "between (or beneath?) the closed eyelids of Siddhartha."

Hira Bansode's other poem 'Slave'[25] aims at criticising male-dominance in the Indian cultural context. She refers to the ill-fated lives of the Indian heroines—Sita, Ahilya and Draupadi—despite their being three of the "Panchkanyas" (Five Daughters) as hailed by the Hindu orthodox tradition, saying:

> Where Sita entered the fire to prove her fidelity
> Where Ahilya was turned to stone because of Indra's lust
> Where Draupadi was fractured to serve five husbands
> In that country a woman is still a slave.

The poem is as much romantic in its expression as realistic in its thematic treatment.

The text, in its parts and even in its entirety, dwells on paradoxes and establishes itself as a poem unveiling hypocrisy and adoption of double standards in the most poetic terms. The sarcasm implied in the last two lines (actually, the one repeating the other) is evident. The poetess seems to infer therein although

> To be born a woman is unjust

Jyoti Lanjewar's poem titled 'The Nameless Ones'[26] reminds one of the relentless struggle that every Dalit has to wage in his lifetime. The dichotomy between the real and the ideal, between life and death is manifest throughout the poem. It asserts one certainty in its concluding lines that carry in their fold an ironic statement, exploding the myth of Tukaram's abhangas that they were restored intact by the river Indrayani when drowned into it. The certainty is:

> the history of pain
> is carved on each of our hearts.
> But even if they could carve words on water
> The Indrayani will not save them.

The poem ends thus on a note of sarcasm coupled with sad indignation.

The next poem, as though in a sequence is "Request"[27] by Anuradha Gurav. It refers to the Hindu custom of offering children, particularly, females, to Khandoba. Such girls after they become major are turned to devadasis, that is, prostitutes for all practical purposes. The poem is an open, severe, attack on the devilish, unethical practice. In the end, the poetess urges:

> Don't wash the stinking rags of our lives
> We are naked already.
> Don't strip us in front of the whole world.

All these poems together may be seen as a new voice of women poets among the Dalits in Maharashtra. In the words of Eleanor Zelliott, "Their voices are strong and varied, echoing other Dalit themes but adding new images, new perspectives, new languages."[28]

To conclude, Dalit poetry may be said to centre around man. Its history of the last twenty-five years or so may be seen in the words of P.S. Nerurkar, the first translator and critic of Surve's poetry, as "the pilgrimage of Mankind towards a brave new world bereft of suffering, suppression and exploitation."[29] For in his poem titled "Karl Marx"[30] Surve rightly announces, as he does in his speech at the gate-meeting:

> now we alone are the heroes of history,
> of all the biographies too—henceforth...

NOTES

1. Arjun Dangle, ed., *Poisoned Bread* (Bombay: Orient Longman, 1992), p. 289.
2. Ibid., p. xiv.
3. See Keshav Meshram, ed., *Vidrohi Kavita* (Pune: Continental Prakashan, 1978), , Introduction, p. 25.
4. Untranslated, available in Narayan Survey, ed., *Sanad*.
5. Arjun Dangle.

6. Kashinath Ranveer, ed., *The Downtrodden India*, a journal, pp. 71-73. Translated by Eleanor Zelliott and others.
7. See K. Satchidandan "Reflections," *Indian Literature*, 158, Nov-Dec. 93, p. 10.
8. Keshav Meshram, p. 29
9. Arjun Dangle.
10. Ibid.
11. Ibid.
12. Kashinath Ranveer, p. 81.
13. Keshav Meshram, p. 21.
14. Arjun Dangle.
15. Ibid.
16. Ibid.
17. Ibid.
18. Ibid.
19. Ibid.
20. Kashinath Ranveer, p. 58.
21. Ibid., pp. 59-60.
22. Ibid., pp. 61-62.
23. Ibid., p. 62.
24. Arjun Dangle.
25. Kashinath Ranveer, p. 65.
26. Ibid., pp. 69-70.
27. Ibid., p. 77.
28. Ibid., p. 80.
29. Narayan Surve, *On the Pavements of Life* (Bombay: Lok Vangmaya Griha, 1973), p. 61
30. Ibid., p. 31.

Treatment of Women in the Fiction of Anna Bhau Sathe

S.D. KHANDAGALE

Anna Bhau Sathe was born on August 1, 1920, in the Mangwada of Wategaon in Walwa Taluka in Sangli District in Maharashtra. Although Anna Bhau was not formally educated, he wrote 32 novels, 22 collections of short stories, 16 plays and folk dramas, a number of poetic compositions and a travelogue. He is one of the few Indian writers who produced such a vast gamut of writings. It was almost for the first time that through his writings the heart-rending portrayal of the sorrows, helplessness and exploitation of the Dalits and the neglected became available in Marathi literature. Therefore, he could rightly be called the bard of masses. He was not only a writer but also an activist of Communist Party of India. Since he wrote about the lives of the oppressed, depressed and neglected, he could be considered as one of the most articulate spokesmen of caste system in India and its disastrous consequences on the Dalits. Initially he was influenced by Marxism but later on came under the impact of Dr. Ambedkar's teachings. During the Dalit literary movement in Marathi, the calibre of Anna Bhau as a gifted writer was acknowledged. His most famous novels *Fakira* (1959) which won Maharashtra State Award for the best literary work in 1961, was dedicated by him to Dr. Ambedkar's warring pen. It was the first Award won by a Dalit literary piece.

Anna Bhau can be described as a philosopher artist. He wrote about almost all strata of society. He wrote about most of the social groups like that of dalits, adivasis, beggars, labourers, criminals, nomads, farmers etc. His writings did not remain restricted only to readers of Marathi, but they spread to the readers of almost all major languages in India and have also been translated into foreign languages like German, French, Russian, Slovak, English and others. In short, he is a writer of enduring fame in Indian literature.

The cause for the writing of Dalit literature is found in the system of Hindu religion. The four-Varna system which gave birth to untouchability is a terrifying force which divided Indian society into thousands of castes which is irrational and grinds humanity remorselessly under its wheels. This system gave a fourth place of Shudra to adivasis, untouchables, other backward classes and women. The Shudras and those far worse than the Shudras were made to live a life of wretched, beggar like homeless and considered them as ignorant, filthy, polluted, inferior sinner and lowliest of the low. Their lot was worse than that of slaves and that slavery had no parallel. Their freedom of mind was destroyed and they were made to live under the state of mental slavery. This casteism and religious fanaticism have had a very pernicious effect on their minds. Preservation of caste-system and untouchability and suppression of women remained the law, culture, religious practice and mentality of Indian religion. No man is basically a dalit or untouchable but this very system deteriorated the life of the downtrodden and made them lead a life of drudgery. The magnitude of deplorable plight of the untouchables was appalling. In short, it is the most artificial social order the world has ever known.

The untouchables in India have been the persecuted and neglected sections of the Hindu social order for centuries. They remained neglected and outcast not only in the Hindu religion but in the Hindu literature as well. The Hindu epics, the *Ramayana* and the *Mahabharata* mainly speak of an oligarchy in which the untouchables had no place. *Manusmriti* of Manu is the manifesto of women's servitude. Therefore, in order to throw off the shackles of slavery of Hinduism and Hindu society and discarding untouchability as a curse or a stigma on humanity, it was Siddharth Gautam Buddha, who tried to give a shock to the rigid caste-system (which was the most important column that supported Hindu religion) by presenting the co-ordination of three principles i.e. Prudence (Pradnya), Compassion (Karuna) and Equality (Samata). He discarded casteism and untouchability and declared humanity as his religion.

In the recent times, it was Mahatma Jyotiba Phule, who tried to voice the problems of dalits and women in his own ways but Dr. Ambedkar's attempts to free dalits from the vampire like clutches of the Hindu caste-system are the most prominent ones in the twentieth century. His attempt to remove the yokes of the caste-system on the necks of the dalits was at a number of levels i.e. social, political, cultural, economic, religious and constitutional. The seeds of the Dalit literature were sown by the struggles and activities of Dr. Ambedkar. Therefore, he could be called the father of Dalit literature. It was his inspiration that set dalits to work with determination and vigour to record their miseries which they were going through for centuries at the hands of Hindu caste-system. Dr. Ambedkar's struggles to free the dalits from the languishing state and the bondages of four-fold classification of the Indian social system had acted as epoch-making milestones. The cultural struggle which took place in Maharashtra through the teachings and philosophy of Dr. Ambedkar for the freedom of dalits gave birth to Dalit literature. Therefore, a number of writers came forward and started ventilating the pains and pangs of the ostracised class of the Hindu society who were denied the basic rights by the Indian social hierarchy, through the various forms of literature.

Dalit literature is a new independent stream which has opened a new trend and enriched Marathi literature. It depicts vividly the miserable conditions and traumatic experiences to which the segregated class of the Indian society was subjected to in the Manu and post-Manu days in India. This school of writing has been the inevitable outcome of the great awakening that took place in India from Mahatma Phule's days down to Dr. Ambedkar. This awakening gave the Dalits a new consciousness and insight into the oppressive system in which they were made to live. This awakening was based on the change and Dalit literature also talks of the change and demands change for the better in the lives of the oppressed masses of Indian society. Therefore, Dalit literature has been the most powerful rebellious expression of the twentieth century. It is also a reaction to the outcast entity thrust upon the Dalits, untouchables, women, nomads, etc.

Although Dalit literature talks of the misery of the caste and class systems, it ultimately aims at a casteless and classless social structure. It firmly believes that man becomes great only if he adheres to the values of liberty, equality, fraternity and social justice and values propagated and advocated by Gautam Buddha like Pradnya (Prudence), Sheel (Character) and Karuna (Compassion). Establishment of a new social order on the principles of these values is the aim of Dalit literature through which the deplorable plight of the Dalits can be brought to an end. Therefore, Dalit literature is not only a literary movement but also a kind of social reformative movement which has a capacity to attract the attention of research scholars all over the world. In short, Dalit literature is marked with the features of revolt and misery since it is closely associated with the hopes for freedom, equality and fraternity of social, economic, cultural and political levels. It is a voice and identity of a perennially deprived and oppressed sections of the Indian social hierarchy. It is essentially a literature of protest against fossilized caste-system.

The level to which Indian women were oppressed in the Indian social system can be seen in *Manusmriti*. Manu gives women a status almost of slaves; she is given a completely inferior place on the ladder of social status. According to Manu, women are physically and intellectually inferior to males; they are weak, sentimental and dependent. Hence, they can never rule. On the contrary, they will always remain a ruled class and they should always obey the males as slaves obey their masters. (Chapter VIII: 416) He further says that women are frail and of weak character. (Chapter II: 213) Manu seems to be thinking that they are a kind of consumable commodity. The paternal family system gave further validity to the slavery of women. Therefore, *Manusmriti* could be taken as a manifesto of women's slavery.

Surprisingly, some of the western philosophers also seem to be toeing Manu's line as far as women's place in society is concerned. Thinkers like Aristotle, in his book *Politics* says that a male is naturally superior to a female and a female is naturally inferior to men. That is why a male dominates a female and she accepts his domination. Further, he defines a woman as an 'impotent male'. Philosophers like Rousseau, Kant, Hegel also seem to be thinking along the lines of Aristotle about the reasoning power of women.

A woman is exploited not only because of her sex but on the basis of her class, race and caste. The plight of dalit women is far more terrible because she is imprisoned in three ways i.e. caste, class and sex. The pangs of neglect, rejection and poverty that a dalit woman is subjected to are unimaginable. Due to the horrible treatment meted out to women in various parts of the world in general and in India in particular, it is essential to take women's liberationist attitude in the interest of women themselves.

On account of such attitude towards women, most of the writers in Marathi upto Anna Bhau Sathe, hardly thought that women could be a subject for their writings—novels or stories. Most of the Marathi Dalit writers wrote about the plight of women depicting their miseries, helplessness, diffidence, inability and exploitation. Among these writers, Anna Bhau occupies a prominent place due to his specific treatment of women in his fictional writings. He depicted women with a difference. He showed that women should not be depicted as unattractive, helpless, incapable and docile. On the contrary, he showed that women also are powerful, capable of protecting themselves and of taking revenge on those who trouble them. He dealt with a number of facets of women's lives in his writings.

Due to Anna Bhau's insight into women's problems and a deep sympathy for them, he felt like portraying their terrible plight through his literature. It is with this conviction that Anna Bhau started writing about women. His portrayal of women is distinct from other writers in Marathi. Contrary to women being portrayed as helpless, weak, exploited and defiant, Anna Bhau depicted them as strong, confident of fighting self-respecting and of good character. He depicted them as capable of freeing themselves from the devilish clutches of slavery at many levels—physical, mental, intellectual and cultural. By doing this, in a way, Anna Bhau was launching a severe attack on Manu who had insulted women.

The women Anna Bhau Sathe treats in his fiction, play a number of roles. The thought, which Anna Bhau introduced probably for the first time in Marathi literature, was that a woman is not an object of sexual pleasure but a life-partner. He has given equal and respectful status to woman. He gives unique importance to the chastity of a woman. The women in Anna Bhau's novels are bold; they face the situations squarely. In an age when most of the Marathi writers showed the women characters continuously weeping over their lot, Anna Bhau showed such women who with their boldness tried to shape their future. Most of the women that Anna Bhau portrays are not immoral. In case they behave immorally, it is not because they like it but because of the compulsions of the circumstances. No woman in Anna Bhau's fiction wants to earn her livelihood or earn a name for herself by deliberately using her body as a medium of earning these things.

Anna Bhau rejected the traditional portrayal of women where it was shown that the women are only to be looked at from a utilitarian point of view. On the contrary, Anna Bhau portrayed his female characters as self-respecting, fighting and self-reliant beings. In his writings, the presentation of the dignity of women has a central place. Although these women came from the disadvantaged classes like dalits, farm-labourers and workers, Anna Bhau tried to show that man-woman relationship should be based on equality between man and woman and also on morality and humanity. Therefore, his female characters seem to be commending the good and condemning the evil. In this attempt of theirs, they don't hesitate to make any kind of sacrifice that is required of them. The female characters in Anna Bhau seem to be as strong, courageous and talented as his male characters. Although these women are bold and fearless, they do not lead wanton lives.

Anna Bhau's female characters are women with pleasant personalities. This kind of portrayal of women has its basis in Anna Bhau's attitude towards women. He looked at women as one of the pure, chaste and attractive creatures. Therefore, he used to say that he does not like uglifying his characters and more specifically female characters. This is the reason why Anna Bhau portrayed women in his writings as attractive persons.

Some of the most important novels of Anna Bhau which deal with women characters are: *Chitra* (Picturesque) *Vaijayanta*, *Chandan* (Sandalwood), *Chikhalatil Kamal* (Lotus in Mud), *Phulpakharu* (Butterfly) *Tila Lavite Mee Raktacha* (I Put Gory Mark on Forehead) which is also entitled as *Aavadi* (Loved and Liked) and *Ratna* (A Gem).

Chitra is entitled after the central character Chitra. This novel shows the demerits of Industralisation that took place in cities like Bombay around 1945-46 and also its effects on the sexual morality of the people. It depicts how flesh-trade boomed along with the increase in industrialisation and how thousands of females were made the victims of flesh-traffickers. Due to the attraction of money even some closest kith and kin forced female relatives into flesh trade. Chitra's story stands testimony to this theme. Her maternal uncle first forces her elder sister, Sona, into prostitution in Bombay and then he tries to do the same with Chitra. But she puts up a stiff struggle and saves herself from selling her flesh, decently marries Jaya, a communist activist and a worker in a factory in Bombay.

Vaijayanta focusses on the problems faced by Tamasha artists. This has been accepted as the first novel in Marathi dealing with this theme. It depicts how particularly female artists in tamashas are sexually, socially, financially and emotionally exploited and how most of them enter this profession out of sheer helplessness. In the novel, we have one Gajarabai who has been a tamasha danseuse for the whole of her life. As she gets old, she is naturally unable to perform her dance with as much agility as he used to when she was young. Consequently, she is publicly insulted and jeered at by another young rival danseuse namely Chandra. Gajarabai has a daughter namely Vaijayanta. In fact, Gajarabai had decided not to subject her daughter to the trials and tribulation that she was subjected to as a tamasha danseuse. But, just to seek revenge of Chandra by defeating her in dancing, she asks her daughter to dance in tamasha performance only once and defeat Chandra. Merely to satisfy her mother Vaijayanta dances and defeats Chandra. Later on out of financial constraints as well as to seek emotional revenge of those who rejected her as a decent woman, she starts dancing regularly. However, after a number of turns, at last she is to be married to one Uma and there is a prospect of a happy end to her life.

In *Chandan*, Anna Bhau depicts the courage shown by Chandan, a workwoman from the slums in Bombay, in order to preserve her physical chastity vis-à-vis the attempts of some villainous characters who are bent upon molesting her. At the age of 12, her maternal uncle wedded her to a labourer. She along with her husband, Jagu, and their son, Raja, come to Bombay in search of employment. But while at work, Jagu dies in an accident and after his death, she has to fight tooth and nail to preserve her physical chastity amidst the villains who wanted to have physical relations with her. The novel is a story of how she fights against these villains. Probably for the first time in Marathi literature a workwoman is depicted in this light.

Fulpakharu is a story depicting the boys in a remand home and their devastating life. Dilip and Gyan, two of the boys from a remand home, deceptively bring Rohini, a village girl, to Bombay falsely promising her a bright future full of jobs and money but actually force her into prostitution when they reach Bombay. It is Dilip, one of the pimps, who describes her as a butterfly to her customer, Jack. She wants to get rid of it. Fortunately one Raja, who stays in the hut opposite to hers in the slum where she stays, shows his readiness to marry her, knowing fully well that she was a prostitute and thereby rescues her from the hell-like life of prostitution.

Alaguj is the love story of Rangu and her lover Bapu Kharwate. Rangu is daughter of a rich and respected farmer, namely, Ganu Mohite. On the contrary, Bapu is very poor and only a servant in Ganu Mohite's house. But Rangu is very fond of Bapu's skill in playing on alaguj (flute). It is this fondness that makes her fall in love with him. After going through the usual ordeals of a love story, at last they succeed in getting married.

Rupa has the usual motion picture-like love-triangle which consists of Rupa (the heroine), Dinkar (the hero) and Gaja Nanagar (the villain). In between these characters lies Mathibai who is a round character in the sense that in the beginning she helps Gaja to get Rupa for him. But when she is beaten by Dinkar and is a failure due to circumstances, she changes sides and starts helping Dinkar and Rupa who wanted to marry and who fulfil their desire in the end.

Aaghat makes use of the flashback technique. It ends with a love affair and registered marriage between Sham and Rosy. It is also a portrait of a Bombay slum with its various facets--criminality, jealousy, lowliness and, of course, good-heartedness. Sham, the central character of the novel, comes to Bombay settles down in a slum, works as a painter, earns enough to cater to his own, and his family's, needs and lives quite happily. But out of feminine jealousy, his neighbour, Takawali, who is a morally lax woman, burns Sham's wife, Rosy. This event gives an unbearable blow to him. However, it is Rosy's love that helps to overcome the blow and to come to a normal way of life.

Murti advocates inter-caste marriages and breaking of caste barriers by the youth. The story of the novel revolves around Vasant, a school-boy and a sensitive parentless artist-painter who falls in love with Murti, his class-mate, a girl from upper-caste. In the end, they get married in spite of being from different castes.

As far as Anna Bhau's depiction of the feeling of love is concerned, he has depicted various facets of love like good and evil, selfishness and selflessness, fighting and slavish lovers, noble, balanced as well as impatient lovers. The characters in these novels are of numerous tendencies like practical, heroic and villainous. Anna Bhau believed that the selfless love touches the very springs of life.

In conclusion, we may say that Anna Bhau Sathe was one of the farsighted writers about the problems of women. This could further be extended by saying that although Anna Bhau was not formally educated and although he did not have the knowledge of recent theoretical/philosophical developments about women's issues, his writing was along the lines of feminist theory.

In a way Anna Bhau intuitively knew what feminism was without knowing that it was developing into a branch of theoretical discipline. This he could do because of his genuine and deep sympathy towards women, their lives and their problems. This also further shows that theoretical training is essential for those who do not have inborn understanding of the problems of the masses. Without any formal theoretical training Anna Bhau could rightly understand the problems of the masses including those of women. This is the hallmark of a real genius which Anna Bhau certainly was.

To my mind, Anna Bhau's treatment of women seems more sympathetic and genuine than the other writers in Marathi literature. It would suffice to say that he believes in chivalry and is very much of a minority in this belief.

NOTES

Bajrang Korde. *Anna Bhau Sathe, Makers of Indian Literature* (New Delhi: Sahitya Akademi, 1999).
Bhalchandra Phadake. *Vedana va Vidroha* (Pune: Shreevidya Prakashan, 1989).
Asaram Gaikwad, *Lokshahir tatha Loklekhak Anna Bhau Sathe* (Nasik: Zep Prakashan, 1996).
Baburao Gurav, *Anna Bhau Sathe, Samajvichar aani Sahityavivechan* (Bombay: Lokvangmaya Griha, 1991).

The Theme of Marginality in Anna Bhau Sathe's Novels and Short Stories

B.S. KORDE

Anna Bhau lived between 1920 and 1969. His place in Marathi writing is significant because at a time when most of the writers in Marathi had not only come from the so-called mainstream classes, but had also been more often than not, writing about the mainstream themes only, it was Anna Bhau who had himself not only come from a marginalised class, i.e. Mang or Matang[1] community, but had also been writing about marginalised groups and themes in Maharashtra society. By writing about varied social subjects in Marathi literature thereby making the centre of this literature move from urban middle class to the marginalised groups like the socially and economically oppressed and therefore marginalised.

The marginal social groups that he depicts are mostly the downtrodden, exploited, backward, ignorant, untouchable and/or dalit[2] groups like that of Mangs, cobblers, nomads, traditional rural artists like dancers, singers in tamasha[3], muralis[4], waghyas[5] and women in general. He also deals with those groups which are marginalised mostly due to economic reasons. Since they are poverty-stricken, they are casteless because poverty itself is their caste. They are people like thieves and dacoits, liquor-traffickers, murderers, slum-dwellers, pickpockets, jailbirds, beggars, prostitutes, pimps, bastards and the like. He also shows marginalisation within marginalisation.

Hence, although there are a number of groups in dalit movement (a movement of the marginalised), no group has denied Anna Bhau's ground-breaking work in the field of *dalit* writing. In fact, he is treated as the first prominent, noteworthy and capable dalit writer. That he was the writer of marginality could also be seen from the fact that he dedicated his most popular novel *Fakira* to the struggle-oriented pen of Dr. Babasaheb Ambedkar who was the most powerful voice of the marginalised in this country, a kind of Martin Luther King of India.

One of the characteristics of the marginalised characters in Anna Bhau's fiction is that although they are marginalised, they do not meekly accept their lot or do not meekly submit to the forces of marginalisation. On the contrary, they fight out the constricting circumstances around them. Their motto seems to be to "change the world with a stroke" which is the first line of Anna Bhau's verse, composition on Dr. Ambedkar's life and mission. He felt that although majority of the human beings in India was marginalised, these marginalised groups, in fact, played a very crucial role in the maintenance and the existence of this earth. That was why he had said at a point that "this earth does not rest on the hood of a legendary serpent *shesha*[6], but on the palms/shoulders of dalit and workers."

Of course, he does not have blind prejudices against all the persons born in the mainstream classes. On the contrary, he acknowledges with gratitude the benevolence and sympathy of some characters from mainstream towards the marginalised ones. It is here, I think, that he looks different from most of the present day dalit writers who, some people say, are seen to be only abusing people from the mainstream.

Some of the prominent examples of his delineation of the marginalised groups and members in these groups are as follows:

Fakira, the most famous of his novels, which was eulogised even by Jnanpeeth Award winning novelist in Marathi namely V.S. Khandekar and which won the Maharashtra State Award for the best literary work in 1961, probably, for the first time in Marathi literature exhibited the power and prowess of a marginalised class of Mangs, a class neglected for centuries. Of course, before Anna Bhau, a writer like S.M. Mate had, through a short sketch entitled "Taralkhoryatil Pirya" (Pirya in Taral Valley) collected in his *Upekshitanche Antarang* (Interior of the Neglected [1941]), tried to show the life and power of the neglected. But it was sketchy. Anna Bhau did it in an elaborate way. Before him hardly had any one done it in Marathi on the grand scale as he did it. Through *Fakira,* he shows noble qualities of the depressed life fighting, rebelliousness, readiness to die while fighting, self-pride and courage to stand by the needy and the deserving through thick and thin.

It is a story of Fakira Ranoji Mang, Anna's real maternal uncle. In his preface to the novel, Anna records that when he was born just a few days' ago, one midnight, riding a horse, Fakira came to Anna's house and from the back of the horse itself inquired about the well-being of the Sathe family. When he was told that a male child (who later on came to be known as Anna Bhau Sathe) was born to his sister, he gave them two handfuls of silver coins which he had looted from the British treasury, asked them to take care of the child and the child's mother and rode away the galloping horse.

Due to famine, fever, epidemics and hunger, the depressed classes were just dying due to lack of food to eat. Vishnupant Kulkarni of Fakira's village asks the depressed to do anything but survive. Encouraged by this advice and coupled with his own tenacity, Fakira loots godowns of grains and exchequers of the British and their henchmen and distributes them among the depressed, the poor and the needy. Hence, I feel that *Fakira* could very well be called a Robinhood story in Marathi. As a result of Fakira's deeds, the Indian-born police officer of the British namely Babarkhan tries his level best to bring Fakira to book. But Fakira absconds, takes refuge in jungles and frustrates Babarkhan's attempts to arrest him. But when his kith and kin are taken hostage and tortured by the British for him, Fakira surrenders and is later on hanged to death by the British. He dies, but leaves behind him an immortal and inspiring story which is at the heart of *Fakira.*

Some of Anna Bhau's best stories are the stories about the marginalised groups/characters. These stories also include such characters who fight on their own or some body else fights for them. One of the noted Marathi writers namely Acharya P.K. Atre eulogised Anna Bhau's stories in this category as follows: "These stories are of those who fight for living. . . . The blood that flows through the veins of them all is of fighter type. Each one of them wants to live honourably. Against offensive forces they apply their full strength with a view to be victorious. . . . Their chests are always ready to receive strokes. . . . Through all these stories Maharashtra temperament is evident."[7] The stories in his first collection, *Khulawadi* (Village/Hamlet of the Crazy Ones), stand testimony to the above-quoted assertions.

Anna Bhau shows that when it comes to the problems of dalits and of social justice, even some non-dalits who are, by and large, known for being peaceful, also take a revolutionary stand. For example, a story in *Khulawadi* entitled "Vishnupant Kulkarni" shows that although Vishnupant comes from an upper caste, i.e. Brahmin, a caste that is well-known, by and large, for living a peaceful, non-revolutionary life gives dalits a revolutionary advice when he sees the worst plight of dalits in his village due to a famine and an epidemic in 1918. His advice to dalits was: "Do anything, but all of you must survive." He meant to say that they should not hesitate even to loot the foodgrain-stores of those who have them in excess and are simply hoarding them. Taking clue from Vishnupant's advice, the dalits loot the foodgrains, a police complaint is lodged against them and they are arrested. But even here Vishnupant almost wages a fight with the law and order machinery and makes them release the arrested ones.

In "Bandawala" (Rebel) we come across a male character from Mang community who stands against injustice. The central theme of the story could be summarised thus: One Inamdar (a landlord/an aristocrat) grabs eighty bighas (hectares) of land of an innocent Mang in exchange for a very paltry amount. For two generations, the land remains in the possession of the Inamdars. Tatya, grandson of the Mang who mortgaged the land, tries to free it from the clutches of the Inamdars. During the course of his attempts to do so, he is sent to jail twice under the fake charges of attempting to beat and murder Inamdar. When all humble and legal ways of getting the land back from Inamdar seem to be useless, at last, Tatya turns a rebel.

"Ramoshi" (A Village Servant from Mang Community) shows how in a quarrel between two arrogant feudal lords the lives of the poor, honest, innocent people are, unnecessarily, crushed, how government machinery has been corrupted and how this plight forces a common, sensitive man to take law into his hands. It is a story of how Yadu Ramoshi, an honest protector of a village namely Maldan, seeks revenge of one Tatya Dongare, a feudal lord and the killer of Yadu's only son, Khandu, of how Tatya absconds, of how Tatya's relatives attempt to grease the palms of law and order machinery, of how, upon hearing all this, Yadu's faith in law and order department vanishes and then of how he himself takes to arms and kills the absconding Tatya in the jungles.

In "Barabadhya Kanjari," a story from which the title of the collection is derived, we get a sketch of the life of a character from a nomadic, uneducated, poverty-stricken community namely *Kanjari*, a community which lives in hutments in slum areas in Bombay. The story also brings with it the worst conditions and inhuman practices that prevail in the whole of the community from which Barabadhya hails. Barabadhya, as per the prevalent practice in his community, sells his daughter, namely Nilli, for Rs. 200 only to one Dallaram to whose son, namely Saidya, Nilli will be married. As per the rule of the community, Nilli is bound to stay in her in-law's house till her death even if her husband passes away. But breaking this rule, young Nilli, after her husband's death, runs away with one Haidarya, a youth who lived in a hut right in front of hers.

When Dallaram comes to know about this development, he holds Nilli's father responsible for her running away and asks him to return the money, i.e. Rs. 200, but Barabadhya refuses to agree to this demand. Consequently, a fight ensues. The court of the caste is summoned which declares Barabadhya to be guilty and asks him to pay back Rs. 200 to Dallaram. And when he refuses to pay, they ostracise him from the community, which means a great harassment to the person concerned, that is, to Barabadhya in this case. But the fighter Barabadhya does not bother about the troubles that are in store for him owing to his ostracisation. The author probably wants to project Barabadhya as a progressive rebel in that community and to show as to how it has been clinging to unjust and outdated practices.

In Anna Bhau's writings, it appears that poverty also functions as a marginalising factor. "Sultan" (Emperor) illustrates this contention. It deals with a person's life-long struggle for and failure in just filling his belly. It is this situation that works towards marginalising him from the normal life. Although the central character of the story was called Sultan, he was actually a penniless, hungry wretch. The story shows that a man strives, ultimately, to fulfil his basic needs like food, clothing and shelter. A common man attempts to lead his life honestly, tolerantly and within the framework of the morals sanctioned by the society. But when he realises that even after doing all this he cannot even fill his belly, the mad hungry person is left with no alternative but to resort to revolt. And when he prepares himself to face the inevitable struggle for existence, he does not meet the killer. The walls of the jails and laws crumble before his revolt and he gets his rights. The author recommends rebellion in preference to meek submission.

At one point Anna Bhau had stated that in this world, at times, reality is unimaginably stranger than fiction. His story "Smashanatil Sona" (Gold in the Graveyard) could very well be a proof of this statement. It is rated as one of the most excellent stories not only among Anna Bhau's stories, but in the whole of Marathi writing as well. The story shows the worst plight of the poor, the uneducated and the unemployed millions of our country. It further shows that poverty and unemployment can force a man to live even by digging out buried corpses, by sifting the ashes of and also by breaking the mortal remains of the cremated/buried bodies in an attempt to find out trinkets of gold that are supposed to be burnt/buried with the dead bodies mainly of the Hindus. By selling out these trinkets on the dead bodies, the central character of the story, namely Bhima, earns his and his family's livelihood since the quarry in which he was employed was suddenly closed down.

One night, while trying to approach a buried corpse, he is attacked by about a dozen wolves. A fight ensues between him and the wolves for the possession of the buried body. The wolves tear out lumps of flesh from his body and when after waging such a fierce fight with the wolves and shooting them away, he approaches the corpse, in a bid to get gold out of the corpse's mouth, his fingers of a hand get caught up in the most tightly locked up jaw of the corpse on the one hand and he is reattacked by the wolves on the other. He fights against the wolves with one hand and tries to free fingers of the other while the wolves tear flesh from his body in the total dark of the night. The scene is likely to shake the readers to their roots and send shivers down their spine. Bhima's misery does not stop here. In fact, it increases when, in a bid to free his fingers of the caught up hand which incapacitates him for any effective manual work. And ironically, he learns that the closed down quarry is reopening the next day. In the light of these horrendous experiences, Anna Bhau seems to be asking: can any fiction be stranger than this reality?

At one more point, Anna Bhau has stated that on rare occasions he has mixed reality with fantasy. His story "Sapala" (Trap) appears to be an example of this statement as far as the plight of the dalits in rural Maharashtra fifty years ago is concerned because some of the fundamental details in the story seem to be unrealistic. It shows as to what kind of commotion was created in rural parts of Maharashtra when due to the appeal made and the consciousness created among the dalits by Dr. Babasaheb Ambedkar, the erstwhile Mahars[8] denied disposal of dead cattle and also gave up eating carrion. It is a story about untouchability and the revolution of the untouchables in a village namely Paragaon, as well as about the attempts of the high-caste villagers to entrap and ostracise the untouchables and about how the untouchables turn the tables on the villagers.

The story seems unrealistic first because the untouchables in Maharashtra are not generally united under one leadership and secondly, because the high-caste villagers in this country generally do not behave as democratically as is shown in the story.

"Upakarachi Fed" (Paying Back Favours) shows how even among the depressed classes the notions of superiority and inferiority were prevalent some time back. In Indian social structure, untouchability was a great infectious disease percolating from the higher cases to the lowest of the low. This story also, like "Sapala," shows the influence of Dr. Ambedkar's movement against the oppression of the depressed classes and of Dr. Amebdkar's attempts of boosting the confidence of these classes.

"Walan" (Deep-Seated Habit) is one more story dealing with various facets of the effects of Dr. Ambedkar's movement for the eradication of social injustice done to the dalits. Dr. Ambedkar's movement was against the deep-seated evil practices, acts, habits and prejudices in the minds and behaviour of non-dalits as well as among the dalits. His movement was an attempt to make all the concerned to part with all that was evil, unpleasant, unhygienic, inhuman and a "basis" for apartheid in India. In consonance with this Dr. Ambedkar had appealed to all the dalits to give up unhygienic and unpleasant habits like eating carrion which was one of the deep-seated habits, due to economic/social compulsions, among most of the dalits of Dr. Amebdkar's times. But many of them found it somewhat difficult to part with that habit. In fact, their behaviour was not exceptional; it was in line with a proverb that says 'old habits die hard'. "Walan" shows how all the Mahars of a village decide to give up eating carrion in response to Dr. Ambedkar's appeal and how one, almost seventy-year-old lady, namely Chima from the erstwhile Mahar community, finds it difficult to quit the deeply ingrained habit of eating the flesh of buffalo.

"Dongaracha Raja" (King of Mountains) in *Jivant Kadtus* also appears under the title "Savala Mang" in another collection entitled *Krishnakathachya Katha* (Stories on the Bank of the Krishna). The same character of Savala appears also in the most popular novel, *Fakira*. Like many other stories, "Dongaracha

Raja" is also set against the backdrop of Indian struggle for independence. It shows how Savala and his associates like Nilu Mang, Fakira, Mura, Pira, Chinchanikar, Ghonchikar, Bali Sajurkar, Bhiva of Khujagaon in Warana valley and some others had revolted against the unjust British law declaring Mangs to be a criminal caste in a bid to prevent them from their probable revolt against and their threat to the British rule in India. The story speaks for Savala's nobility of head and heart, for his courage, moral uprightness, sympathy for the oppressed and antipathy towards the oppressor. Savala is shown to be having all these virtues in him in spite of the fact that as per the caste-ridden Indian social structure, he is given a position on the last rung of the ladder of social status.

In "Farari" (Absconding), we have a brave and sentimental central character namely, Shiva Mang. His father-in-law, Yemaji Mang, is villainous. Shiva and Yemaji quarrel with each other. In this belligerent mood, he goes to the shoemaker of his village whom he had paid Rs. 2 only in advance, i.e. four months before, for making a new pair of chappals. But the shoemaker had, still, not made them. Consequently, Shiva is enraged. He was already angry with his father-in-law and now the shoemaker has also insulted him by not making the pair of chappals and also by speaking arrogantly. An enraged Shiva beats the shoemaker severely and then absconds fearing arrest. However, he is arrested, tried and sentenced to twelve years of imprisonment. After he is released from the prison, he finds that his family life is in a mess. His father-in-law has forced his daughter, i.e. Shiva's wife, Yesu, to marry somebody else and resultantly, she has begotten a child by her second husband. After coming out of the prison when Shiva finds this, he goes to Yesu and since their love was very deep, he brings her back although she had married some other fellow and had delivered baby by him. The story is probably intended to show that those who beat and murder others are also human beings and therefore sentimental and sensible. They turn beaters and murderers not because they like it, but because of the compulsion of circumstances.

Like "Ramoshi" in *Kulawadi,* "Savala Mang" in *Krishna-kathachya Katha,* "Farari" in *Jivant Kadtus* and in *Swapnasundari,* "Nilu Mang" in *Jivant Kadtus* is a pen-portrait of a courageous but basically a humble person. Through Nilu Mang it is shown how dishonesty of some persons like Chimaji Patil and Ramu Sutar makes a basically decent man like Nilu Mang a criminal and how he again behaves decently when he is forgiven for his crimes which he had committed not for his personal gains but only for teaching the scoundrels a lesson. However, the ending of the story, wherein it is shown that the officers of the British government then in power cancel Nilu' sentence—of killing him by tying him to the mouth of a gun and then firing the cannon-ball seems unrealistic and unconvincing.

NOTES

1. An "untouchable" caste or a member of the caste. In ancient times they were supposed to be employed as executioners, hired murderers etc.
2. A term used for the depressed, the deprived and the erstwhile "untouchable" classes in India.
3. A diverting performance or play comprising song, dance, mock-fight etc. The most popular folk art form of Maharashtra.
4. A female dedicated to the god Khandoba at Jejuri in Pune district of Maharashtra. She does not marry throughout her life as she is supposed to be married to god Khandoba.
5. A male counterpart of *murali*, that is, a male dedicated to the god Khandoba at Jejuri.
6. A huge legendary serpent supposed by traditional-minded Hindus to be holding the earth on its hood.
7. P.K. Atre, "Introduction," Anna Bhau Sathe, *Khulawadi* (Bombay: Abhinav Prakashan, 1957).
8. An "untouchable" caste or a member of that caste in western India, particularly Maharashtra.

Awakening Social Consciousness: Mulk Raj Anand's *Untouchable*

R.K. DHAWAN

Mulk Raj Anand has been described as a novelist with deep social commitment. A close study of his works shows that he juxtaposes the social evils against the mindsets of individuals and some privileged sections of the society. In *Untouchable*, he has chiefly dealt with the ghastly evil of untouchability afflicting the Hindu society of the pre-Partition era, in the larger backdrop of the caste-configurations within the Hindu society that have successfully stifled the healthy growth of a considerable section of Indian community for centuries.

Anand has vividly depicted in the novel the miserable lot of the unfortunate untouchables and suggested that they can be freed from the shackles of killing orthodoxy and tradition only if men infuse into their own hearts some sympathy and tenderness and if the men who are humiliated as pariahs muster enough courage to live boldly and healthily.

Untouchable has no story interest; it is just an impassioned plea for a social cause. And it is this singleness of purpose i.e. exposing the evil of untouchability and analysing its various aspects—social, moral, psychological, religion-based, etc.—that provides structural unity to the plot. The plot of *Untouchable* can, unmistakably, be hailed as one of the most compact and coherent plots in Indian English fiction. This view finds confirmation in the fact that getting convinced of the advice of Mahatma Gandhi, Anand reduced the size of his manuscript to almost half of the original, keeping out extraneous details. In his well-known essay "On the Genesis of *Untouchable*," Anand observes:

> In retrospect, I feel that, under the tutelage of the Mahatma, who did not pretend to be an artist, I was able to exorcise all those self-conscious literary elements which I had woven into the narrative in anticipation of what the critics might approve. He thought that the paragraphs of high-sounding words, in which I had tried to unite the miscellaneous elements, in what was essentially a walk through the small town of my hero, must go. Also, the old man suggested the removal of my deliberate attempts at melodramatic contrasts of the comic and tragic motifs, through which the spontaneous feelings, moods and lurking chaos in the soul of Bakha, had been somewhat suppressed.
>
> And the Mahatma asked for the deflation of those clever tricks, which had made the expression of concrete detail into a deliberate effort at style.
>
> Out of two hundred and fifty pages, hundred and fifty were left.[1]

Observing the three Aristotelian unities, though unconsciously, the novel records a day's events in Bakha's life which serve as a mirror to the pathetic condition of the untouchables who form the lower stratum of society in the caste-ridden orthodox Hindu society, especially in the pre-Partition times.

The harsh reality portrayed in the novel figuratively and artistically is the process of alienation and frustration that has been unleashed because of the various pigeon-holes into which the Hindu society is getting divided. As has been appropriately observed by E.M. Forster in the preface to the novel:

> The sweeper [untouchable in this case] is worse off than a slave, for the slave may change his master and his duties and may even become free, but the sweeper is bound for ever, born into a state from which he cannot escape and where he is excluded from social intercourse and the consolations of his religion. Unclean himself, he pollutes others

when he touches them. They have to purify themselves, and to rearrange their plans for the day. Thus he is a disquieting as well as a disgusting object to the orthodox as he walks along the public roads, and it is his duty to call out and warn them that he is coming. No wonder that the dirt enters into his soul, and that he feels himself at moments to be what he is supposed to be.[2]

The opening paragraph of the novel epitomises the 'big divide' between the untouchables and other resident communities in the town:

The outcastes' colony was a group of mud-walled houses that clustered together in two rows, under the shadow both of the town and the cantonment, but outside their boundaries and separate from them. There lived the scavengers, the leather-workers, the washermen, the barbers, the water-carriers, the grass-cutters and other outcastes from Hindu society. (9)

The novel begins with an autumn morning in Bakha's life. He is in bed, half-awake, "covered by a worn-out greasy blanket, on a faded blue carpet which was spread on the floor, in a corner of the cave-like, dingy, dark, one-roomed mud-house." (10) It is so early that the sun has not risen.

Bakha is the son of Lakha, the 'Jemadar' of all the sweepers in the town and the cantonment. His chief duty is to keep the three rows of public latrines clean. These latrines are used by men from both the town and the cantonment. Bakha has for sometime worked in the barracks of a British regiment. He had looked at the Tommies, with wonder and amazement when he first went to live at the British regimental barracks with his uncle. He had had glimpses, during his sojourn there, of the life the Tommies lived: sleeping on low canvas beds covered tightly with blankets; eating eggs, drinking tea and wine in tin mugs; going to parade and then walking down to the bazaar with cigarettes in their mouths and small silver mounted canes in their hands. And he had soon become obsessed with an overwhelming desire to live their life. He knew they were white sahibs. So he tried to copy them as much as he could in the exigencies of his peculiarly Indian circumstances. His father had been angry at his extravagance, and the boys of the outcastes' colony teased him on account of his eccentric dresses and called him 'Pilpali sahib'. And he knew, of course, that except for his English clothes, there was nothing English in his life.

As he is still lying in his bed, Bakha hears his father's stern and authoritative call, "Get up, ohe you Bakhya, ohe son of a pig!" (13) He is angered at the abuse as he is already feeling depressed that morning. His father's abuses create a growing dislike in his heart for the short-tempered, sickly old man. But he has fond memories of his mother and thinks of the days when she was alive. She showed him all the affection that warmed his heart. She used to give him a brass tankard full of a boiling hot mixture of water, tea-leaves and milk from the steaming earthen saucepan. It was so delightful, the taste of that hot, sugary liquid, that Bakha's mouth watered for it on the night before the morning on which he had to drink it.

Bakha comes out of his reverie as he hears the shouts: "Ohe, Bakhya! Ohe, Bakhya! Ohe, scoundrel of a sweeper's son. Come and clean a latrine for me!" (15) It is Havildar Charat Singh, the famous hockey player of the 38th Dogra regiment. He suffers from piles and accuses Bakha for his ailment: "Why aren't the latrines clean, ohe rogue of a Bakha? There is not one fit to go near. I have walked all round. Do you know you are responsible for my piles! I caught the contagion sitting on one of those dirty latrines!" (16) Bakha picks up his brush and basket and sets out to clean the latrines.

Though his job is dirty, Bakha remains comparatively clean. He looks intelligent, even sensitive, with a sort of dignity that does not belong to the ordinary scavenger, who as a rule is uncouth and unclean. The Havildar is thoroughly impressed by Bakha's quickness and efficiency in doing his job: "You are becoming a 'genterman', ohe Bakhya!" (17) With a grin which symbolises two thousand years of racial and caste superiority, he asks Bakha to see him that afternoon and take the gift of a hockey stick from him.

Bakha feels grateful at this gesture on the part of one of the best hockey players of the regiment. Charat Singh's generous promise calls forth that trait of servility in Bakha which he has inherited from his forefathers: the weakness of the downtrodden, the helplessness of the poor, the passive contentment of the bottom dog, suddenly illuminated by the prospect of fulfilment of a secret and long-cherished desire. He salutes his benefactor and bends down to continue his work again.

When he gets to the end of his work in the third row of latrines for the second time during the morning, he feels a cramp in his back and stretches himself out from the bent posture he has maintained all the while. After the process of cleaning the latrines in the final fourth round, he feels extremely exhausted but he is intuitively reminded of his next job.

The real ordeal for Bakha begins when he goes into the town to sweep the streets as a substitute for his father who has said that he was not feeling well. Bakha is not only scolded but also slapped by a Hindu merchant who alleges that Bakha has touched him and thus polluted him.

A strong believer in the dignity of man and equality of all men, Anand is naturally shocked by the inhuman way the untouchables are treated by those that belong to superior castes—especially the Brahmins or the so-called "twice-born." The degradation and humiliation inflicted on the unfortunate sections of society is highlighted through the oft-repeated refrain of Bakha 'Posh, posh, sweeper coming.' The very fact that they were not allowed to mount the platform surrounding the only source of drinking water in the town of Bulandshahr called 'the caste-well' and had to wait sometimes for hours together for the generosity of some caste-Hindu to pour water in their empty pitchers, speaks volumes about how deep-rooted this evil had become. Although Bakha and his other outcaste friends sometimes played hockey with the two boys of the Hindu babu, yet the mere touch of a caste Brahmin unleashes an invasion of abusive epithets and physical assault on Bakha. He had purchased the mouth-watering jalebis and is lost in enjoying the taste of eating a portion of them when he unconsciously touches the tunic of a caste Hindu who immediately starts shouting:

> Why don't you call, you swine, and announce your approach! Do you know you have touched me and defiled me, cock-eyed son of a bow-legged scorpion! Now I will have to go and take a bath to purify myself. And it was a new dhoti and shirt I put on this morning. (51)

Coming out of his reverie, Bakha is completely taken aback and his hands instinctively join together in apology without uttering a single word. He only bends his forehead over them and mumbles something but the 'touched' man does not care to hear what he says as he is not satisfied with Bakha's dumb humility. He again starts abusing him:

> 'Dirty dog! Son of a bitch! offspring of a pig!' he shouted, his temper spluttering on his tongue and obstructing his speech, and the sense behind it, in its mad rush outwards. 'I . . . I'll have to go-o-o . . . and get washed-d-d . . . I . . . I was going to business and now . . . now, on account of you, I'll be late.' (51)

The situation results in a crowd gathering round to see what the row is about and this encourages the aggrieved man further in his denunciations. Says this man: "This dirty dog bumped right into me. So unmindfully do these sons of bitches walk in the streets." (52) Bakha stands motionless, with a hopeless expression of meekness on his face. The entire crowd gathered there forms a circle round Bakha, but takes care to keep at a distance of several yards from him. They all are on the side of the man who has been complaining about Bakha's misdemeanour. Bakha feels as if he will collapse. Bakha feels further confused by this fresh development and the novelist describes his misery, hopelessness and helplessness in these words:

His first impulse was to run, just to shoot across the throng, away, away, far away from the torment. But then he realised that he was surrounded by a barrier, not a physical barrier, because one push from his hefty shoulders would have been enough to unbalance the skeleton-like bodies of the onlookers, but a moral one. He knew that contact with him, if he pushed through, would defile a great many more of these men. And he could already hear in his ears the abuse that he would thus draw on himself. (52)

A street urchin who has just joined the crowd says that this sweeper-boy, namely Bakha, has been beating small innocent chaps like himself. When he protests against the false accusation and asks for forgiveness for his present crime of 'forgetting to call his arrival' and 'touching the caste-Hindu', no one in the crowd believes a word of what he says. The crowd feels absolutely no sympathy for Bakha. Rather the onlookers take a sadistic pleasure in watching him in distress. The peculiarity of his problematic situation is echoed aptly in these observations of Anand:

He was really sorry and tried hard to convey his repentance to his tormentors. But the barrier of space that the crowd had placed between themselves and him seemed to prevent his feeling from getting across. And he stood still while they raged and fumed and sneered in fury: 'Careless, irresponsible swine!' 'They don't want to work.' 'They laze about!' 'They ought to be wiped off the surface of the earth!' (54)

It is only a passer-by Mohammedan tonga-wallah who shows sympathy towards him. This sympathy infuriates the 'touched man' further who gives Bakha a harsh and sharp slap on the face and it results in his turban falling off and the jalebis in the paper bag in his hand getting scattered in the dust. This unfortunate incident makes him indulge in pitiable self-analysis of his plight in this interior monologue:

> Why was all this fuss? Why was I so humble? I could have struck him! And to think that I was so eager to come to the town this morning. Why didn't I shout to warn the people of my approach? That comes of not looking after one's work. I should have begun to sweep the thoroughfare. I should have seen the high-caste people in the street. That man! That he should have hit me! My poor jalebis! I should have eaten them. But why couldn't I say something? Couldn't I have joined my hands to him and then gone away. The slap on my face! The coward! (56)

He becomes acutely aware of his low social status and protests in his mind:

> The cruel crowd! All of them abused, abused, abused. Why are we always abused? The santry inspictor that day abused my father. They always abuse us. Because we are sweepers. Because we touch dung. They hate dung. I hate it too. That's why I came here. I was tired of working on the latrines every day. That's why they don't touch us, the high-castes. (56)

He is moved by the kindness of the tonga-wallah but the word "untouchable" haunts him:

> The tonga-wallah was kind. He made me weep telling me, in that way, to take my things and walk along. But he is a Muhammadan. They don't mind touching us, the Muhammadans and the sahibs. It is only the Hindus and the outcastes who are not sweepers. For them I am a sweeper, sweeper—untouchable! Untouchable! Untouchable! That's the word! Untouchable! I am an Untouchable!' (56-57)

Bakha now becomes acutely aware of his being an untouchable and begins to announce "Posh, posh, sweeper coming" (59) as he starts walking. With booming rage in his mind, he asks himself why he was treated in such an abusive and insulting manner by the Hindus. He also wonders why the sahibs and Muslims don't mind touching them. The cruelty and orthodoxy of the Hindus is thus sharply focussed. These factors, the novelist seems to hint, are the probable reasons for conversion of a large number of low caste Hindus to Christianity.

After roaming around aimlessly, though fascinated by the stalls where the brass band musical instruments are displayed, Bakha goes to the temple where he is to sweep the courtyard. The sight of the stone deities from a distance (as he is not allowed to enter a Hindu temple) seem to calm his troubled mind. Driven by his curiosity to know more about the caged snake-god, he climbs a few steps leading to the holy place inside. Deeply moved by the rhythmic singing there, he instinctively folds his hands as if to worship inwardly the unknown god. He hears just then a loud cry "polluted, polluted, polluted!" (67) This runs a wave of shock among the devotees. Bakha thinks he is undone, having come so near the deities.

Just then, Bakha catches sight of his sister Sohini standing at a short distance from him. As he goes near, the crowd also closes in, shouting that Bakha had defiled the holy precincts. Sohini tells him a different story altogether. While she was cleaning the lavatory of the priest's house, the priest had tried to outrage her modesty. When she protested and screamed, he came out of his place shouting that he had been polluted by her touch. The priest had not only disgraced Bakha's sister but had also attracted the sympathy of the crowd by accusing him of having polluted the premises.

Though he feels much troubled at heart, Bakha realises his helplessness; he can do nothing to expose the hypocrisy of the priest. He takes hold of Sohini and they walk towards the outer gate of the temple in order to go home. On the way, however, he realises that he too was fully aware of his sister's charm and he hated the very idea of her being married to a stranger. The next moment he feels a wild desire to retaliate when the thought of the priest's action returns to him. But realising his helplessness, he wishes that his sister were not beautiful.

As they approach the outcastes' colony, Bakha is reminded that his father has asked him to collect food for the family. Asking his sister to go home, he himself goes to the silversmiths' colony. He shouts: "Bread for the sweeper, mother; bread for the sweeper." Feeling tired and defeated, when no one responds to his requests, he sits down on the wooden platform of a house and, leaning against the door, falls asleep.

Bakha sees a dream now where he finds himself on a railway platform. There is a train consisting of a large number of wagons loaded with goods of all kinds. Then he imagines himself in a small village with narrow muddy streets with cows wandering about and two big carts stuck in the mud. He also sees himself in the compound of a school where boys are reading aloud.

As his dream continues, Bakha suddenly hears loud words, "Alakh, alakh," the shouts of a half-naked sadhu and the women coming out with chapatis and dal for the holy man. A housewife becomes furious when she sees Bakha on the threshold of the house and scolds him "Perish and die" as he has defiled her house. Bakha asks for her forgiveness and appeals for food. After a lot of fuss, she flings a chapati as if giving it to a dog. Bakha's tolerance now reaches the nadir and he returns home with only two chapaties and does not know how he would explain the situation to his old father. He is uncertain whether he should inform his father what had happened to him and Sohini in the town. But he is unable to make up his mind.

The old man calls him a good-for-nothing scoundrel and expresses the hope that his younger son Rakha might bring something nice to eat from the barracks. Bakha's mind travels to those days when he used to get plenty of food from the Hindu families and the degrading incidents of the morning engulf him. Seeing him lost in thoughts, his father feels that something is wrong. Bakha gives a poignant account of all that had happened to him and Sohini and tells his father that he would not go to the town again. Lakha consoles his son impressing upon him the hopelessness of their situation and asks him that he had taken care not to abuse any Hindu and not to hit back at any stage. He then narrates an incident how during Bakha's acute illness in his childhood, he had been ill-treated at the Hakim's house and also how the Hakim had later visited their house in the outcastes' colony to save dying Bakha's life.

When his younger brother Rakha comes with some food from the barracks, they all start eating from the same basket but Bakha suddenly stops when his hand touches something sticky in the pieces of the left-over chapaties and his mind is filled with a sense of revulsion that it might be mixed up with somebody's saliva. He excuses himself from eating by telling a lie that he had been invited by Ram Charan to his sister's marriage where he will receive his share of sweets.

Bakha reflects in an interior monologue his early association with Ram Charan's sister and his desire to marry her. But the girl's mother Gulabo thought it below their dignity and had taken two hundred rupees from another person for the hand of her daughter. Being washermen, they considered themselves superior to Bakha in the hierarchy even among the outcastes.

When he reaches near the place of the marriage, he meets his other friend Chota and cannot muster enough courage to join the marriage festivities. But having been seen by Ram Charan, both of them call him out so that they can go for playing hockey for sometime. However, Bakha starts behaving in a strange manner. Lost in his thoughts, he does not respond to their jovial behaviour. On learning about unhappy and disgusting experiences of the morning, both Chota and Ram Charan express sympathy with him and wonder if they could catch hold of the swine-like pundit to kill him on the spot. However, they realise that this will be impossible and futile. Ram Charan and Chota now ask him to get the hockey stick from Havildar Charat Singh and promise to return soon for the play.

Another aspect of untouchability is unfolded by Anand through the kind of treatment meted out to Bakha and other outcastes by the Mohammedans, Christians and the men in the armed forces. If Bakha is humanely consoled by the Mohammedan tonga-wallah after he is slapped by the touched-Lalla, Havildar Charat Singh too offers him tea and gives him a hockey stick. The nobility of the medical profession is also held high through the unexpected visit of Hakim Bhagwan Das to Lakha's house when Bakha's condition had deteriorated to the extent of impending death.

On his way to Charat Singh's house, Bakha once again sees with longing eyes at a sola hat hanging in the quartermaster's room of the 38th Dogras. He had always longed to own that kind of hat and had even thought of stealing it somehow but the fear of the alert sentries makes him change his mind.

When he ultimately meets Charat Singh, he finds that the latter is a broad-minded person who offers him tea and gives him the promised hockey stick. Bakha is filled with deep gratitude for Charat Singh for his kindness and leaves the barracks in a happy mood.

On the way, Bakha meets the military babu's two sons who also want to play hockey. The younger son is not allowed to play as they feel that he might get hurt during the game. In fact, the younger son does get hurt and is carried by Bakha when he is still bleeding profusely. The Babu's wife is surprised to see her injured son and accuses Bakha of defiling her house by coming there. This confuses his mind and infuriates his heart. In a dejected mood, he returns to the playfield to find that all the boys have gone home. After hiding the hockey stick among the bushes, he starts trudging towards his home.

Bakha is ill-treated by both his father and younger brother for wasting his time instead of engaging himself in the job of cleaning the latrines in the barracks. When he is told to leave home, Bakha is filled with utmost despair. He starts wondering what he had done to deserve the misery he was experiencing. He says that he would rather prefer dying to being ill-treated both at home and outside.

Towards the end of the novel, Anand seems to suggest a few solutions to this evil of untouchability. One of these refers to the efforts being made by the Christian missionaries through their local Salvation Army, the head of which is one Colonel Hutchinson. According to him, Christianity and Christ stand for equality of all human beings. In an answer to Bakha's constant questioning as to who Christ was, the Colonel says: "He sacrificed Himself out of love for us. . . . He sacrificed Himself to help us all; for the rich and the poor; for Brahmin and the Bhangi." (142) Bakha seems to feel that in Christianity, there is no difference between 'the pundit of the morning' who thought himself defiled and polluted by his touch, and a sweeper-boy or bhangi like him. But the question of the Original sin and all human beings being sinners baffles him. Bakha is overwhelmed by the foreigner's interest in him but is unable to understand what he is told about the love of Christ, the Original Sin and other related stories. He also cannot bring himself to accepting conversion to Christianity for the sake of equality.

The rude behaviour and insulting remarks about the sweepers made by Colonel Hutchinson's wife fill Bakha's mind with pain once again and he starts moving aimlessly when he suddenly hears some people shouting "Mahatma Gandhi ki jai" followed by another group shouting still louder "The Mahatma has come!" Along with the crowd of people, he too goes to the Golbagh where Mahatma Gandhi is going to address a meeting. Here in this sea of humanity, he finds people from all classes and castes together as if Gandhi was a magnetic force to bring the much-needed equality for all and the eradication of the evil of untouchability. He finds the Hindu Lallas, the Kashmiri Muslims, the Sikh rustics, red-cheeked Afghans, Indian Christians and many people from the outcastes' colony together in the crowd. He realises that it was only Mahatma Gandhi who could bring unity among all the castes. But he also feels that

> There was an insuperable barrier between himself and the crowd, the barrier of caste. He was part of a consciousness which he could share and yet not understand. He had been lifted from the gutter, through the barriers of space, to partake of a life which was his, and yet not his. He was in the midst of a humanity which included him in its folds, and yet debarred him from entering into a sentient, living, quivering contact with it. Gandhi alone united him with them, in the mind, because Gandhi was in everybody's mind, including Bakha's. Gandhi might unite them really. (151)

Fortunately Gandhi is speaking on the evil of untouchability in the Indian society in that meeting.

He overhears some babus talking about Gandhi being a legend and the freedom becoming a reality soon under his leadership. He also learns that Gandhi had been released from the jail on the condition that he would not make any political speech. As a Congress volunteer puts it rather authoritatively: "The government has allowed him out of gaol only if he will keep strictly within the limits of his propaganda for harijans for the removal of untouchability." (155)

Just then there arises a shout from the crowd "Mahatma Gandhi ki jai! Hindu, Mussulman, Sikh ki jai! Harijan ki jai!" and he sees the little man escorted by Kasturba Gandhi on one side and his English disciple now called Miraben, on the other. During the course of his speech, Gandhi clarifies:

> As you all know, while we are asking for freedom from the grip of a foreign nation, we have ourselves, for centuries, trampled underfoot millions of human beings without feeling the slightest remorse for our iniquity. For me, the question of these people is moral and religious. When I undertook to fast unto death for their sake, it was in obedience to the call of my conscience. (160-61)

During his speech, Gandhi declares untouchability to be the greatest blot on Hinduism and says that it was very strange for Indians to seek freedom from the grip of a foreign nation while they themselves were trampling upon millions of their fellow human beings for centuries. Then he relates the story of the scavenger boy Uka, an untouchable, for whose sake he always pleaded with his mother in his childhood. The Mahatma expresses the wish to be born a scavenger in his next life so that he could realise their misery in toto and talks of removing the social evil of untouchability. He then exhorts the untouchables to give up their evil habits of drinking alcohol and eating meat. He asks them not to accept the remains of the food from the high caste Hindus but to insist on payment in sound foodgrains. He also expresses the opinion that all public wells, temples, roads, schools and sanatoriums must be declared open for the untouchables. Gandhi concludes his speech with the words: "May God give you strength to work out your soul's salvation to the end!" (164)

Bakha is deeply touched by the concluding words of the Mahatma's speech which seemed to convey Bakha's own feelings of horror and indignation at the ill-treatment of the untouchables by the caste Hindus. When the Mahatma leaves, people again shout, "Mahatma Gandhi ki jai" but he also hears a dissident voice that says that Gandhi is a humbug, a fool and a hypocrite. He voices his disgust about Gandhi living in the ancient times without realising the benefits that could accrue to India from modern technology.

Iqbal Nath Sarashar, a young poet, and his friend R.N. Bashir, a Barrister-at-Law, now discuss how the Indian society can be rid of its bane of untouchability. They talk of introducing the flush system for sewage disposal and recognising equal rights, privileges and opportunities for everyone as was the case with the legal system. They think that the introduction of the flush system will automatically put an end to this obnoxious social evil. As Sarashar says:

> Well, we must destroy caste, we must destroy the inequalities of birth and unalterable vocations. We must recognise an equality of rights, privileges and opportunities for everyone. The Mahatma didn't say so, but the legal and social basis of caste having been broken down by the British Indian penal code, which recognises the rights of every man before a court, caste is now mainly governed by profession. When the sweepers change their profession, they will no longer remain Untouchables. And they can do that soon, for the first thing we will do when we accept the machine will be to introduce the machine which clears dung without anyone to handle it—the flush system. Then the sweepers can be free from the stigma of untouchability and assume the dignity of status

that is their right as useful members of a casteless and classless society.

However, there is no definite and final solution to this deep-rooted social evil which seems to have eaten into the very vitals of the caste-ridden Hindu society. Therefore it cannot and does not lend itself to any easy solutions within the fixed parameters and the novel seems to have done a yeoman's service in highlighting the theme of untouchability in all its multi-faceted perspectives through its open-endedness.

Bakha feels bewildered and his mind is filled with gloom once again when he is left alone. The conflict in his mind makes him more miserable and he makes up his mind to go home and seek some solace by relating the story about Gandhi's visit and his speech to his father. As E.M. Forster says in the Preface: "Some readers may find this closing section of the book too voluble and sophisticated, in comparison with the clear observation which has preceded it, but it is an integral part of the author's scheme. It is the necessary climax, and it has mounted up with triple effect." (8)

The plot of *Untouchable*, though linear in form and simple in content, is perhaps one of the best experimental plots in the elementary stage of Indian novel in English. The use of the narrative techniques of stream-of-consciousness, flashback, reverie, interior monologue etc. and confining the action to less than twenty-four hours in the life of its hero Bakha makes it one of the most well-structured plots. The single-purpose theme of untouchability, being defined and analysed from different viewpoints and in all its complexity, provides it the much-desired coherence as is clear from Anand's observation:

> The binding together, the orchestration, and the interplay of Bakha's inner feelings and outer experience, with the apperception of the intangible "cloud of unknowing" hovering over his head, was not achieved merely spontaneously. The different elements had to be knit together, with intense effort, to achieve some sort of coherence. (Dhawan, 12)

Though *Untouchable* does not have the conventional form of a proper beginning, middle and end, it does have a conclusive open-endedness offering three probable solutions to the removal of the evil of untouchability viz. conversion to Christianity, Gandhi's exhortation to the Harijans to shun the bad habits and get integrated into the mainstream of the Indian nation slowly but surely, and the introduction of the flush system. In this connection, Forster's observation in the Preface to the novel is quite relevant:

> The book is simply planned, but it has form. The action occupies one day, and takes place in a small area. The great catastrophe of the 'touching' occurs in the morning, and poisons all that happens subsequently, even such pleasant episodes as the hockey match and the country walk. After a jagged course of ups and downs, we come to the solution, or rather to the three solutions with which the book closes. . . . Bakha returns to his father and his wretched bed, thinking now of the Mahatma, now of the Machine. His Indian day is over and the next day will be like it, but on the surface of the earth if not in the depths of the sky, a change is at hand. (7-8)

NOTES

1. Mulk Raj Anand, "On the Genesis of Untouchable: A Note," *The Novels of Mulk Raj Anand*, ed. R.K. Dhawan (New Delhi: Prestige, 1992), p. 11.
2. Mulk Raj Anand, *Untouchable* (1935; New Delhi: Orient Paperbacks, 1970), pp. 6-7.

The Crisis in Human Values in Mulk Raj Anand's *Coolie* and Arundhati Roy's *The God of Small Things:* A Comparative Study

ROSY MISRA

Throughout the ages literature has always explored human values and their relevance in moments of crisis. This is especially evident in Indian writing in English, which from its very beginning has focused on social issues. In this context a comparison between Mulk Raj Anand's *Coolie* and Arundhati Roy's *The God of Small Things* is of particular interest, for the two writers are very different. Not only is one a male the other a female, they belong to different socio-historic periods and areas of interest. Anand established himself in the first half of the twentieth century, he is one of the pioneers of Indian fiction writing in English, being classed with R.K. Narayan and Raja Rao as the founders of the Indian novel in English. But Roy is a contemporary novelist—young and volatile. Anand has been greatly influenced by Marxism, Roy is emphatically not a Marxist. Nevertheless, their novels are comparable on various levels. Both are revolutionary novels and depict the social reality of conflict between the powerful and the powerless, and treat the downtrodden humanistically. Both are social reformers.

When I was reading *The God of Small Things*, the picture of Munoo came to my mind again and again. *Coolie* is what one might call a character novel with the focus on one person being victimised by society. But in Roy's novel, all the characters are victimised in some way or the other, in a perpetual repetition of what has been happening through time. In Munoo's story, amorous love is almost absent whereas in *The God of Small Things* the main thread of the story is a love affair between a high-caste Christian woman and an untouchable. In spite of these differences, the novels are comparable on various levels. They are sagas of conflicts between the powerful and the powerless. This paper attempts to compare the encroachment upon human values and the resultant crises which lead to the tragic deaths of the main characters of both the novels.

Coolie (1936) portrays the yawning gap between the haves and have-nots, the exploiters and the exploited, the rulers and the ruled, the powerful and the powerless. It is a veritable saga of unending pain, suffering, and prolonged struggle punctuated only occasionally by brief moments of relief and hope. Beginning his journey from the house of his loveless uncle and aunt, Munoo passes through diverse situations—as a domestic servant in an urban middle-class family in Sham Nagar, as a worker in a small pickle factory and as a coolie fighting for work in the city market in Daulatpur, as a labourer in a cotton mill in Bombay and as a rickshaw coolie in the employ of an Anglo-Indian woman of no morals. Before he dies, Munoo is subjected to exploitation at the hands of various exploiters in four different places.

In *The God of small Things* (1997) Roy presents the tragic plights of several characters being exploited in the hands of various exploiters. It is all about how the human values of children, youth, women, and the untouchable have been encroached upon, and how they have been victimised, and, unwittingly, some of them victimise each other. It tells us a story of an intense, but doomed love affair between a high-caste Syrian Christian woman Ammu and an untouchable Paravan Velutha. We can hear the voices of various victimised characters: the voice of Mammachi, the bitter, long-suffering mistress of the household who was being regularly beaten with a brass flower vase by her husband; the voice of Baby Kochamma, who had been denied love by Father Mulligan, with whom she fell in love; and the voice of Margaret Kochamma the English woman whom Chacko had married. We also hear the voices of the small children, Estha and Rahel, who had been forced to become false witnesses against their friend Velutha. But the voices of Velutha and Ammu, the protagonists, end in their tragic deaths. There is nobody to help Velutha in his crisis. The whole humanity had turned against him. It was Ammu who had initiated their lover affair. The inevitable had happened and Velutha's father Vellya Pappan dutifully informed Mammachi what he had seen. Instead of protecting his son, he asked God's forgiveness for having spawned a monster and even offered to kill his son and thereby destroy what he had created. The "Man-less, Father Mulligan-less Baby Kochamma"[1] was actually jealous of the young lovers' physical union and wondered how Ammu could stand the smell of a Paravan. The crisis was triggered by the drowning of Sophie Mol. On the pretext of saving the family reputation, Baby Kochamma locked up Ammu in the Ayemenem house and informed the police "a few days ago he [Velutha] had tried to, to . . . to force himself on her niece" (259) and kidnapped her children. Velutha was informed by a communist comrade that the police had been searching for him. He directly went to Comrade K.N.M. Pillai for help. Pillai was more worried about the reaction of the people. He told Velutha to his face that Party was not constituted to support worker's indiscipline in their private life. He made it clear that individual's interest was subordinate to the organisation's interest. Velutha did not get any support from the party of which he had been a sincere worker. He was also denied justice in the hands of his employer Mammachi, who instead spat on his face. Ultimately he was arrested by the police and died in the police custody.

Ammu is portrayed as a tragic figure, a woman struggling against her family, her motherhood and society and with herself. Her broken marriage, her unwantedness in her parental family, her love for his children and her womanly desires, lead her to her untimely death. The right to love a man of her choice is a woman's birth right and this birth right of Ammu is encroached upon in the name of caste. Hers is a story of the helplessness of the powerless against the powerful.

The novels under consideration have epic qualities. The four tragic episodes which make up Munno's tragic life—as a servant in bank clerk's household, as a worker in a pickle factory in a feudal city, as a factory worker in an industry in Bombay, and lastly as a servant of a half-caste woman at Shimla—present a sequence of events suggestive of the poor conditions of a helpless illiterate Indian. In a sense he conforms to the archetype having mythic significance for humanity as a whole. *Coolie,* epical in sweep and panoramic in purview, pictures the effects that pervasive evil of class system has on a poor little boy. The novel is remarkable for the largeness of its canvas, the multiplicity of its characters and variety of its episodes. However, the focal point is always Munoo and pathos is sustained by the emphasis on the innocence of Munoo against the merciless, mechanical rhythm of society. Anand humanises the 'coolie'—as in Bakha he humanises the 'untouchable'—and gave him feelings, a mind, a heart, a soul and raised his dignity as a trembling piece of flesh and blood, worthy of commemoration in serious literature. By raising an ordinary wretched creature to the level of a hero, perhaps for the first time in Indian English literature, Anand proves that the struggle of a waif could be as good a subject for a work of art as the Trojan war itself.

In *The God of Small Things,* Roy, with a masterstroke of reversal, draws a parallel between the murder of Velutha in police custody and the murder of Dushasana and Duryodhana at the hands of Bhima. "Another morning, another stage, another kind of frenzy." (235) With this parallelism between Bhima and Velutha, the novelist raises the latter to the status of an epic hero. As far as the theme of crisis of human values is concerned, the parallelism has great significance. In both the stories, there is a struggle between good and evil. In the *Mahabharata,* Dushasana and Duryodhana represent evil and Bhima represents good. Good is able to destroy evil. In *The God of Small Things,* in the struggle between good and evil, evil turns out to be victorious. Velutha who represents good is defeated by the police who represent evil. In ancient India, human rights of the weak were always protected. But in modern India, human values are encroached upon. The police who are servants of the State of democratic set up, the police who stand for Politeness, Obedience, Loyalty, Intelligence, Courtesy and Efficiency, killed an innocent man without even probing the real facts only because he belonged to the downtrodden class. Velutha is, as his name signifies, as white as whiteness itself. Even when he knows that his end is imminent, he remains a true apostle of non-violence. The story of Velutha can be interpreted as an extended allegory of Christ's life. Like Christ he is a very good carpenter, like Christ he remains non-violent. And, again, like Christ, he dies saving other people—saving the reputation of Ammu and her family. Like Christ, he knew that sacrificing his life was too big a cost for this purpose. But he embraces it willingly. When he was taken to the police station, Rahel notices that the nail of his right thumb was painted red. This symbolises the blood of Christ which was shed for others. In this extended moral allegory of struggle between good and evil, Baby Kochamma plays the role of Judas who betrayed Christ. According to this allegory, Velutha achieves the status of an epic hero.

There are many other themes in the novels which are comparable; for instance the themes of incest, child abuse and Oedipus complex are common to both the novels. In *The God of Small Things*, incest is between the twins who meet after twenty-three years. "Only that once again they broke the Love Laws. That lay down who should be loved. And how. And how much." (328) In *Coolie* we find that Mrs. Mainwarring is sexually attracted towards Munoo, who is as young as her son. When Munoo met with an accident under the car of Mrs. Mainwarring, he was physically and mentally broken and felt sad, bitter and defeated, like an old man. "But to Mrs. Mainwarring, he was not the old man he felt himself to be, otherwise she would have had no use for him and would perhaps have left him where she had found him. . . . He was to her a young boy with a lithe, supple body, with a small delicate face and with a pair of sensitive eyes"[2] comments the novelist. She appointed him as a page, for a boy of fifteen was just what she wanted. There are many passages in the novel, which proclaim Mrs. Mainwarring being incestuous or even a child abuser.

The child abuse near the beginning of *The God of Small Things* in the Abhilash talkies by a cold drinks vendor is disgusting. This physical abuse is later parodied in the mental seduction of the children by Baby Kochamma which is blood curdling.

Similarly, the Oedipus complex can also be traced in both the novels. In *Coolie* between Munoo and Parbati—the wife of Seth Prabha Dayal. When Munoo falls sick and is laid up with fever, she nurses him tenderly like a mother and never ill-treats him. But later the warmth of Parbati's body as he nestled against him, aroused the confused feeling of son and lover. "He pressed her close to him. He felt quivering. . . . And for a moment, he forgot himself in her warmth. . . . And his blood boiled with love that crushed him with a torture." (135) In *The God of small Things* the son-lover relationship is between Mammachi and her son Chacko, a divorcee. Mammachi is the Jacosta of *The God of Small Things*. "The day that Chacko prevented Pappachi from beating her, Mammachi packed her wifely luggage and committed to Chacko care. From then onwards, he became the repository of all her womanly feelings. Her man. Her only love." (168) The narrator also emphasises several times how Mammachi takes special care for her son Chacko's room for the "objects of his Needs" (169), "a Man's Needs." (168)

The mingling of fact and fiction is another comparable element in both the novels. All the places through which Munoo moves are geographically traceable. More than that, 'He [Anand] took for his hero his childhood play mate Munoo, who was consigned to labour in a pickle factory and who accepted his lot with a fatalism peculiar to the Indian peasantry.'[3]

Likewise in *The God of Small Things* Roy took the liberty to change Aymanam—a village geographically a ten-minute drive from Kottayam city, to Ayemenem. The Booker prize has unleashed a torrent of interest centring on Ayemenem and the media has been preoccupied with identifying the novel's characters with real life counterparts. The character of Ammu is apparently modelled on Mary Roy—Arudhanti's mother. 'I am not Ammu. Arundhati has created a character called Ammu, using my biodata on her bare bones,'[4] explains Mary Roy. Similarly Arundhati's brother, Lalit Kumar Christopher Roy, has been mistaken by critics as Estha of the novel. The fusion of history and fiction is another similarity. The plight of Munoo and his kind is the direct result of British rule, and of the industrial revolution their rule initiated without consideration for social reforms. One of the highlights of *Coolie* is the Hindu-Muslim feud. Munoo is the horrified witness of communal murder and senseless killings. 'In Indo-Anglian fiction *Coolie* perhaps is the first novel to touch on this subject; and it foreshadows the murderous riots that followed the partitioning of India in 1947.'[5] Further, the episode of the invitation of Mr. W.P. England to Nathoo Ram's house for tea illustrates Anand's conviction that the British Government not only exploited the country's natural resources, but also debased the characters of those Indians who were in its service. It created a body of sycophants, looking upto the English, fawning, cringing, becoming a ready tool of exploitation in the hands of their masters. Nathoo Ram, Dayaram and Todar Mals have been dehumanised in the service of English. This is best seen from the way they bully and abuse Munoo. The police are shown more as a symbol of British oppression than British justice. Their world is a world of hysteria, one without restraint or self-respect. When Prabha goes bankrupt the police yell, shout abuses, fight among themselves for what little might still be got from auctioning the property, and then together fall upon their victim.

In *The God of Small Things*, there is similar hysteric unrestrained and even more cruel attitude being adopted by the police, even several decades after India had achieved independence. This is proved from the way they torture Velutha like animals fall upon their prey. "If they hurt Velutha more than they intended to, it was only because any kinship, any connection between themselves and him, any implication that if nothing else, at least biologically he was a fellow creature—had been severed long ago." (309) There are references to Communism in the chapter 'Pappachi's Moth.' Rahel recognises Velutha who was taking part in a march which had been organised by Travancore-Cochin Marxist Labour Union to present a Charter of Peoples Demands to Comrade E.M.S. himself. The main demands were an hour's lunch break for the paddy workers, increase in women labourer's wages from Rs. 1.25 to Rs. 3.00 and men labourer's from Rs. 3.50 to Rs. 4.50 a day. They were also demanding that untouchables no longer be addressed by their caste names. Instead of Achoo Parayan, or Kelan Paravan or Kuttan Pulayan, they should be addressed as Achoo, or Kelan or Kuttan. (69) There are references to the facts of political history of Kerala. There are also references to Kathakali being performed. Some of the characters like Chacko and Baby Kochamma are representatives of Indian people who were over influenced by western culture.

In *The God of Small Things*, a number of characters are victimised by society. Velutha and Ammu are denied the right to choose their life partners. Ammu had been ill-treated and deserted by her Bengali husband and afterwards by her own people. Velutha's human right to 'relive' as a touchable was encroached upon and he was denied protection of his family, employer and the political party he belonged to. He was denied justice at the hands of the police although he was innocent. They both met with their tragic end. The twins were forbidden love even by their own mother. Estha was treated as a football being returned to his father and re-returned to his mother. Apart from this, his unlucky experience with the cold drink vendor reduces him into a dumb boy. Mammachi had suffered all the evils of a patriarchal family set-up. Love was denied to Margaret Kochamma and even to Baby Kochamma. Thus, in Roy's novel the crisis is caused because human values of several individuals are encroached upon and they unwittingly encroach upon the human values of others.

In *Coolie* also, we come across scores of characters but as far as the breach of human values is concerned, Munoo is the focal point. What he wished for was minimal; to live, to know and to work. But even these basic human rights were denied to him. Like the twins of *The God of Small Things*, Munoo became an orphan at an early age and was denied by fate the right to be loved. Like Estha he had to face child abuse at the hands of Mrs. Mainwarring. Instead of caste struggle as in the case of Velutha, he had to face class struggle. In Munoo's case, it is only the exploiters that change, the exploited remains the same. Thus as far as suffering is concerned the character of Munoo is an amalgamation into which several of Arundhati Roy's characters like Velutha, Estha, Rahel and even Ammu culminate.

Both Anand and Arundhati are social reformers in their own way. Munoo's tragedy seems to be Anand's plea for reform. 'Beneath this pervasive pessimism, there is an essential undercurrent of optimism in that the protagonist's death poignantly establishes the rotten state of society and the consciousness of the need for its drastic reform.'[6] Similarly, Roy also emerges as a prophetess of the new millennium—prophetess of gender and social equality. She seems to plead never to forget about the small things in life: the insects and the flowers, wind and water, the outcast and the despised.

NOTES

1. Arundhati Roy, *The God of Small Things* (Delhi: IndiaInk, 1997), p. 45.
2. Mulk Raj Anand, *Coolie* (New Delhi: Arnold, 1988), p. 285.
3. Saros Cowasjee, *Studies in Indian and Anglo-Indian Fiction* (New Delhi: Harper Collins, 1993), p. 50.
4. Qtd. in Venu Menon, "Sleepy Aymanum," *Outlook*, Vol. III, No. 44 (New Delhi, 1997), p. 126.
5. Cowasjee, p. 65.
6. K. Venkata Reddy, *Major Indian Novelists* (New Delhi: Prestige, 1990), p. 12.

Black Identity in Selected Novels of William Faulkner

K.S. IYER

The three novels I have chosen are *The Sound and the Fury,* published in 1929, *Absalom, Absalom!* published in 1936 and *Intruder in The Dust,* published in 1948. From the perspective of New Historicism which, essentially, contemplates the, 'textuality of history and the historicity of the text,' the three novels can be squeezed into the history of racialism from the Civil War (1861-65) time to after the end of the Second World War. This history is the major text from which the three novels draw their historicity vis-à-vis the 'certainty' of their plots.

Historically, *Absalom, Absalom!* belongs to the period of the American Civil War in the context of which much of the action takes place. *The Intruder in the Dust* belongs by virtue of its action, to the 1920s. *The Sound and the Fury* covers a period of thirty years, ending in 1928, at the vestiges of the World Depression of 1929-30. All the three novels trace the gradual degeneration of the South for several common and particular reasons, incorporated in the plots of novels. One reason for regrouping the three novels so as to appear as a trilogy is that, in all the three novels the doctrine of racial and human equality operates with variations on the theme. Secondly, the continuance of the process of dehumanization of the black race from the time of the Civil War in which the Southerners suffered a rout, threatening the very existence of the blacks, to the time in history in *The Sound and the Fury* in which Dilsey, the Negro servant transcends racial and other barriers. Thirdly, poverty, which was rooted in the history of the blacks since their migration to America, denigrates the race to a status lower than that of the white pigs in the homes of the white men. Fourthly, the psychological feeling of compunction in the minds of the blacks, generated and sustained by their feeling of belonging to an inferior race, which drove the members of the race to harbour an inveterate psychosis of fear of extinction. Fifthly, the contemplation of their own accursed plight which no good can help ameliorate, led the blacks to derive vicarious pleasure from the hatred of the whites. The aforesaid causes operate in some form or the other in these novels, but the saving grace can be seen in the efforts of some one or the other of the characters to endure and strive to unite the two races.

To begin with *Absalom, Absalom!*. The protagonist of the novel, Sutpen was affronted by the liveried black servant of a rich white plantation owner, when Sutpen, the poor white, was a boy of ten. He had gone to the 'big house' to communicate to the owner of the House his worker-father's message. He was told by the black servant that he could not come to the front door of the planter's House, but had to go around to the back of the House because he was a poor white! For several years Sutpen embarks on a quest for riches and through foul means, more than fair, comes by property and a wife whom he rejects with her son, when he learns that she is an octoroon. He provides enough money for mother and son and comes to own, as he had long desired, a big house called Sutpen Hundred.

Thomas Sutpen, secure in his 'Hundred', desires to have a white son as his heir. He marries the mild Ellen, daughter of a local good man, Coldfield who had assisted him, in some questionable way, to become the owner of the Hundred. He gets a son Henry and daughter Judith. Henry goes to Harvard, where he meets Charles Bon, whom he befriends, brings home for Christmas, intending him to be his Sister's husband. Judith and Charles fall in love and when the father is informed he objects to the union, when he learns from Charles' antecedents that he is his own son, his mother being the Octoroon he had deserted earlier in his life. The Civil War breaks out, in the meanwhile, and Henry learns of Charles' antecedents and confirms his father's suspicion of Charles' Negro-blood.

On return from the War Henry invites Charles to his house and kills his half-brother, whether connived at by his father or not, one cannot certainly say; then Henry absconds, lives in his own house in secrecy for four years or so and then dies. Sutpen is thwarted in his design of a white heir to his property by his son's death and even a part-white heir is beyond his reach, with Charles' death. The major question in this novel is, therefore, miscegenation. It is clear that Henry killed his half-brother Charles whom he loved, more to prevent miscegenation, than incest. Thus, the major question is racialism, the inhumane basis, on which the novel's later action stands. Sutpen offers marriage to Rosa Coldfield, younger sister of Ellen, after Ellen's death, on condition that she gives birth to a son, after which only will the marriage be solemnised. Rosa spurns the offer and Sutpen is stalked by his nemesis in his effort to find a male white heir. Finally, he is killed by his white servant, Wash Jones, for failing to acknowledge the latter's grand-daughter Milly as his wife because she delivered a baby girl!

The immediate cause of the tragic events, in the novel, that resulted in the failure of Sutpen's design was his refusal to recognise his part-Negro son Charles. The question of black identity that the novel projects is a kind of positive chance to uplift the blacks. Sutpen brings about the downfall of the Old South, with his own downfall, when faced with a chance he chose to destroy "rather than admit brotherhood across racial lines." [Hyatt Waggoner, *Past and Present: Absalom, Absalom!*] In Sutpen's tragedy, the villain of the piece is the system of slavery—an institution Faulkner frequently called a "curse." The unnaturalness of this system is embodied in the fact that it blinds Sutpen to the reality of natural kinship and leads to fratricide. Faulkner, significantly, employs the title of the novel to suggest in clear terms, the similarity with the biblical account of David the father and Absalom, the son—the latter slays his half-brother Ammon for committing incest with their sister, Tamar. David said, "My

Son" to Absalom, even after Absolom's rebellion, but Sutpen would not say it to Charles—so deep was his racialism.

Sutpen's racialism and his pride in his whiteness is shown and mocked at by Faulkner when he describes Sutpen fighting with his slaves, stripping himself naked to the waist only to prove himself and incidentally to his slaves, "that he is the better man." (Cleanth Brooks, *History and the Sense of the Tragic: Absalom, Absalom!*) At the end, Faulkner hopes fervently, for a reconciliation based or founded on a footing of equality between the two races. Judith, Sutpen's daughter, acknowledges blood kinship with Charles'—her half brother's—son. "Judith is one of Faulkner's finest characters of endurance—and not merely through numb, bleak stoicism but also through compassion and love. Judith is doomed by misfortunes not of her making, but she is not warped and twisted by them. Her humanity survives them" [Cleanth Brooks, *History and the Sense of the Tragic: Absalom, Absalom!*]

In the final analyis, Sutpen, in trying to attain equality with the white master of his father, by owning a Big House, ironically surrenders that equality, by leaving at death an idiot, black great grandson as his heir! Secondly, and also ironically, he has his revenge against the black, liveried servant who refused admittance to him from the front, by preventing his own black (part-black) son Charles' admittance in his family. Thirdly, Faulkner seems to say that the multiplication of the population of the impoverished, revengeful, whites-hating blacks, has been the result of the historical misdoings of the whites in their promiscuous, sexuality, perpetuating the very race they had hated.

Intruder in the Dust depicts the deep-rooted uneasiness and the erratic violence of assertion, involved in Negro-white relationship. The novel has a murder, a threatened lynching, a lonely and risky trip in the night to a graveyard, a close-race with racialism and the status of the Negro, but it is a positive step forward from *Absalom, Absalom* towards Faulkner's search and discovery of black identify.

In the novel, an old Negro with white blood, Lucas Beauchamp, is alleged to have killed a white man, Vinson Gowrie.

Lucas is arrested and is to face trial. He is sure to be convicted, as it always happened, and it is feared that before he appears in the court, he will be lynched by the whites.

Lucas once helped a white young boy of sixteen who had fallen through ice. The white boy is Charles or Chic Mallison. Lucas, even, gave him food. When Charles offers money for saving him, Lucas disdains the payment as an insult to his prestige as a man of social position. While the white boy's people have their conventional views about a Negro or part-white Negro, Lucas, throughout his life, challenges Mallison to set aside his conventional views of what a Negro is and to treat him as a man, instead. In the novel Lucas is pitted against the white boy and the novel's happenings are presented from the white boy's point of view. "The real theme is the relation between the two." [Edmund Wilson, *William Faulkner's Reply to the Civil Rights Program*].

When Lucas is arrested, Mallison wants to show to Lucas what he, as a white man must be to Lucas, a part white Negro. Lucas doubts that (though he fired the pistol) he killed the white man. He commissions Mallison to go to the graveyard and with the Sheriff's help exhume the dead body of the white man to ensure whose bullet killed the man. Finally, it is established that the white man's own brother killed him and the whites wanted to implicate the good, old, part-white Negro, Lucas. For the whites, even the life of an utterly bad white man was more precious than that of a good Negro. This attitude was a natural outcome of their belief in the white's racial superiority.

From the beginning, till the end of the novel, Faulkner makes Gavin Stevens, the white Lawyer for Lucas, to make statements bringing out the reasons for the backwardness, distrust and hatred of the Negro by the white race. The gist of the reasons advanced are:

(a) a passive acceptance by the Negroes themselves of the idea that, being Negroes they were not supposed to have facilities to wash properly, to be clean;
(b) a Negro was not a human being,

(c) a Negro like Lucas was an old, friendless, opinionated, arrogant, intractable hard-headed intractable, independent, insolent Negro and so he was certainly a murder, even without evidence.

As the novel concludes, Mallison, the white boy comes round to re-evaluate the Negro's status—he moves from label and cliche to recognise Lucas as human. In the novel, "the Negro must be saved [Faulkner seems to be saying] so that the white can become his moral equal, be relieved of the bondage to his terrible mistake." "Lucas' innocence is proved by a sixteen-year-old boy. The boy had been haunted for years by his feeling that he was in debt to Lucas . . . for having eaten part of the old man's dinner." [Elizabeth Hardwick, *Faulkner and the South Today*]

As Edmund Wilson argues: "The Negro is homogenous too" as the Southern whites are. "The saving remnants of Southerners (Whites) such as the characters in the novel who rescue Lucas, should combine with the non-second-rate Negro. . . . Let the white man give the Negro his rights, and the Negro teach the white man his endurance" and together they would dominate the United States. [Edmund Wilson, *William Faulkner's Reply to the Civil Rights Program*] This seems to have been Faulkner's vision, in the novel, of a future America.

In *Intruder in the Dust* and the other two novels, where Negroes have central or important roles, "What Faulkner does" according to Frederick J. Hoffman, is to make the characters transcend his (or her) sufferings qua Negro, to emerge not as Negro but as man—man, that is beyond complexion and ethnic considerations. The final story is never one of the social injustice. . . but of an existentialist's struggle of the will to affirm itself." [Chapter 5: *The Negro and the Folk*] In the novel, Faulkner acknowledges the Negro's moral victory over the South. This perception of the final emancipation of the Negro is real and historical. Symbolically, by his help, the white boy grants Lucas, the Negro, his selfhood, his identity.

The Sound and the Fury is set in the background of the Great Depression of 1929-30, which had begun to have its toll upon many prosperous, American Southern families of which the Compson's is one specific instance. The novel traces the gradual disintegration of this family from 1898 to its sudden crash in 1928, with Quentin Jr. running away with the circus man and all the money that Jason, her uncle had saved over the years. The causes of the decline of the family, have been the moral decline of the members of the family, the cynicism of the father, the hypochondriac mother's neglect of her children, the eldest son Quentin the shadow of the truly heroic protagonist, who quits the novel in the middle of action, the daughter Candace's sexual promiscuity and her daughter reliving her mother's life, Jason's misanthropism resulting from his materialism and the love-starved idiot son Benjy left to fend for himself.

But this is only the outer frame of the novel. The real story is the story of Dilsey, the black servant of the family for many years. Dilsey in the novel is a woman who belongs to the marginalised class—the Negro. She is the eternally suffering but enduring and forgiving black woman who, despite all odds against her, finds her identity.

In the novel, Dilsey is not, as James Baldwin interprets, "the comforting illusion of black forgiveness" nor is she what Irving Howe calls the "historically unavailable moral archetypal model." But, for Faulkner, she is the forlorn hope, both of the whites and the blacks of the modern age. She is the closest answer to the black riddle. She is no slave, though riddled by poverty and ignorance. In her, inequality of the two races and the identity crisis are submerged and resolve themselves into a state of spiritual ascension. "The Easter Sunday Service in the Negro Church is immensely moving, an apotheosis of simplicity, innocence and love, with Dilsey and Benjy as the central figures." [Michael Millgate, *The Sound and the Fury*] As Ralph Elison has said: "Faulkner began [his novel-writing] with a stereotype of the Negro and ended with creating human beings." This remark truly applies to Dilsey, who as Faulkner affirms in his Nobel prize Acceptance Speech: "Will not merely endure . . . will prevail. [She] is immortal, not because [she] alone among creatures has an inexhaustible voice, but because [she] has a soul, a spirit capable of compassion and sacrifice and endurance."

NOTES

Cleanth Brooks, *William Faulkner—The Yoknapatawpha County* (New Haven: Yale University Press).
Frederick J. Hoffman, *William Faulkner* (New York, Twayne, 1961).
Irving Howe, *William, Faulkner: A Critical Study* (New York: Vintage, 1963).
Robert Penn Warren, ed., *Faulkner* (Twentieth Century Views, N.J.: Prentice Hall, 1966).

Motherhood in Toni Morrison's *Beloved*

BHARATI A. PARIKH

Toni Morrison's 'narratives' have put forth disturbing questions before the society—readers, scholars, 'community' and critics alike. Being an imaginative writer that she is, with firm roots in the Afro-American tradition, intensity of feeling and probing mind to examine socio-economic, political, cultural problems during and after slavery, Morrison disturbs and enhances our understanding of Afro-American life during as well as after the Declaration of Emancipation in *Beloved*.

Her technique to recapture the past, mingle it with the present, not to name or number the chapters of her novels, render her work complex. The power to name her people, which will evoke the hardships borne by black in and out of slavery commands our respect and inspires awe of her matchless craft.

Beloved is an adjective, commonly used by one and all. Yet, in the novel *Beloved* (1987), Morrison once again brings out the essence in naming the lost, murdered daughter of Sethe, the slave woman of "iron eyes and backbone to match." The terrible ordeals borne by mothers during slavery come alive through the narrative in *Beloved*. The novel also deals with lives of blacks as was lived during plantation era, hence some call this novel written in the plantation tradition. On one hand, we see how Morrison bestows dignity to blacks who were all called 'men' by the plantation owner Mr. Garner, who prided himself in doing so, when majority of plantation owners considered their slaves as 'property'. All men are named alike, Paul, with the variation of last initial, e.g. Paul D. Garner, Paul A. Garner, Paul F. Garner, Mister, Halle Suggs, and Sixo, the tough man.

Thus, there lies the mockery of the system evolved by the whites for keeping slaves as their property, unmindful of Afro-Americans as persons and their entity as human beings. As Scruggs suggests, naming is "an existential act that manifests a vital community whose space is fluid, protean." (171) Even the laws formulated by whites did not proclaim humanity of the blacks. Compared to Morrison's earlier novels, *Beloved* is a historical novel set in the nineteenth century. Though an imagined narrative, it is based on a particular incident in the past.

As the novel unfolds, the first sentence evokes a sense of mystery: "124 WAS SPITEFUL. Full of baby's venom. The women in the house knew it and so did the children. For years each put up with the spite in his one way, but by 1873 Sethe and her daughter Denver were its only victims." (3)

The sheer helpless condition of blacks during and after Emancipation reveals their strong sense of place. Be it a house as in *Beloved*. "The place where Sethe lived, didn't have a number then." (3) It was the gray and white house on Bluestone Road on the outskirts of Cincinnati. During slavery, most black women "were not, by and large, domestics in the house," contrary to popular impression, rather, they were labourers in the fields with the men. It also "meant that the women were deprived of houses, of being householders." (qtd. Scruggs, 172) Naturally, these circumstances led Morrison's women strongly attached to houses, even those that seem cursed. Besides individual well being and sense of identity, Morrison is concerned with the community, which needs to support the individual in a society where survival of women was so hard, as in *The Bluest Eye* or *Sula*, or even in *Song of Solomon*. Thus, in *Beloved*, Morrison evinces "the redemption of the house, the origins of community, and the integration of the individual within the community's life-sustaining body." (Scruggs, 173)

Beloved was awarded the Pulitzer prize. It concerns the "awful, lingering effects of slavery on black mothers" (Payant, 196). The story was stimulated by a contemporary newspaper clipping telling of a Kentucky runaway slave, Margaret Garner, who tried to kill her children at the home of her mother-in-law in Cincinnati, rather than have them go back to slavery as noted in *Newsweek* by Clemmons. The story commands utmost attention by taking into its fold all the issues an Afro-American writer must envisage. As Alice Walker projects: "A womanist writer will recognize that, along with her consciousness of sexual issues, she must incorporate racial, cultural, national, economic and political considerations into her philosophy." (qtd. Payant 166) Morrison's writings lay bare the experiences of black women, who "are the touchstone by which all that is human can be measured." (Ibid)

The two fingers of mother in the novel naturally arrest our attention. Baby Suggs celebrates Sethe's reunion with the family along with her four grandchildren. Morrison is deeply interested in the strength of blacks in surviving, not only surviving but in the "wholeness of entire people, male and female." Halle had bought freedom for his mother after five long years of hard work. She lived "sixty years a slave and ten years free." (104) These were her last words before she died. But when she was freed, she reached the outskirts of Cincinnati. Baby Suggs had been a beacon of light to the entire community. At the time 124 had been "a cheerful, buzzing house where Baby Suggs, holy, loved, cautioned, fed, chastised and soothed." (87)

It is ennobling how through her own experience of slave life, she had attained a deep understanding of travels of the blacks. After emancipation, she wanted to build a strong community of blacks. Because slave life had "busted her legs, back, head, eyes, hands, kidneys, womb and tongue, she had nothing left to make a living with but her heart—which she put to work at once." (87) She was the best loved and sought after among her people. She reinvents herself, her being and inspires others to follow suit. Thus, Baby Suggs attains 'becoming' from the state of being. Her largeness of heart is described thus: "Accepting no title of honor before her name, but allowing a small caress after it, she became an unchurched preacher, one who visited pulpits and opened her great heart to those who could use it." (87)

Thus, the nurturing quality of the mother/ancestor in Baby Suggs is symbolically portrayed. The lesson she learnt and taught to all—men, women and children was "love your heart." (89) The men were asked to 'dance' before their wives and children, women were asked to 'cry' and children were told to 'laugh', so that their mothers hear them laugh.

Ceremoniously, she asked all her people to love their own selves, as the whites don't love them; in parts or as a whole. Hence: "You got to love it. This is the flesh I'm talking about here. Flesh that needs to be loved. Feel that need to rest and dance; backs that need support, shoulders that need arms, strong arms I'm telling you. And O my people, out yonder, hear me, they do not love your neck unnoosed, and straight. So love your neck, put a hand on it, grace it, stroke it and hold it up." (88-89)

Baby Suggs advocated loving their heart above all the other parts because "this is the prize." Thus, her plea is replete with compassion for her brethren. Then she danced sunlit dance in the "Clearing—a wide-open place cut deep in the woods nobody knew for what the end of a path known only to deer and whoever cleared the land in the first place." (87)

Later on, when her daughter-in-law, Sethe, joins her, Baby Suggs provides her ample consolation. She tells her to lay all misery, sorrow and shock of losing her husband Halle aside. Nine years ago, Baby Suggs soothed her by "pressing fingers and the quiet instructive voice." (86) Thus, a sort of defence mechanism was developed among black women to stand by each other, as white slave catchers to catch the runaway slaves perpetually haunted them.

Exactly twenty-eight days after the arrival of Sethe at 124 Bluestone Road, Baby Suggs's "faith, her love, her imagination and her great big old heart began to collapse." (89) The picture totally changes at 124, after nine years when "Baby Suggs, holy, proved herself a liar, dismissed her great heart and lay in the keeping-room bed roused once in a while by a craving for color and not for another thing." (89) The mystery of this changes lies in a shocking, indescribable agonizing experience, wherein

"Those white things have taken all." Baby Suggs had or dreamed and broke her "heartstrings too."

As a result of a terrible happening: ... 124 shut down and put up with the venom of its ghost. No more lamps all night long, or neighbors dropping by. No conversations after supper. No watched barefoot children playing in the shoes of strangers. Baby Suggs, holy, believed she had lied. There was no grace—imaginary or real." (89)

Thus, the long coveted dream of a happy reunion comes to a halt. The shock proves too deep for Baby Suggs who lead a life suspended between "the nastiness of life and the meanness of the dead, she couldn't get interested in leaving life or living it." (4) Her past had been 'intolerable' like her present. She had eight children. "Everyone of them gone away from her. Four taken four chased." (4)

It is after eighteen years Paul D. Garner visits Sethe and learns about Baby Sugg's death. She died "soft as cream." For her being "alive was the hard part." The baby ghost of Sethe's daughter, Beloved, haunted the house. After Sweet Home plantation was taken over by school teacher and his two nephews, Sethe's life is annihilated: "The one who had nursed her (taken away her milk) while his brother held her down." (150) "She was Halle's girl. Pregnant every year including the year she sat by the fire telling him [Paul D] she was going to run. (9)

Among the six men at the sweet Home, Sethe was the only female. When she sent her three children from Kentucky to Halle's mother near Cincinnati, Ohio, on a wagon, along with Ella and other women:

> "I had milk" she said, "I was pregnant with Denva but I had milk for my baby girl. (9)

After eighteen years when the last of the Sweet Home man Paul D visits Sethe, she recalls her past. She had planned to join her children soon after they were shot. "Anybody could smell me long before he saw me. And when he saw me he'd see the drops of it on the front of my dress. Nothing I could do about that. All I knew was I had to get my milk to my baby girl. Nobody was going to nurse her like me. Nobody was going to get it to her fast enough, or take it away when she had enough and didn't know it. Nobody knew that she couldn't pass her air if you held her up on your shoulder, only if she was lying on my knees. Nobody knew that but me and nobody had her milk but me. I told that to the women in the wagon. Told them to pout sugar water incloth to suck from, so when I got there in a few days she wouldn't have forgot me. The milk would be there and I would be there with it." (9)

The dialogue charged with mother love, frantic eagerness, and expectancy to see and suckle the baby, oozes out of every syllable. As blacks were not allowed to possess anything, neither relationships nor any belongings whatsoever, Baby Suggs does not hurry to thank Lord when three children arrive safe with the wagon, but no sign of Sethe or Halle. This very baby girl, when the schoolteacher with one nephew, one slave catcher and a sheriff arrive on 124, the house seems too quiet, they suspect that they have reached too late. There had been celebration with "steely old black man," Stamp Paid's "two buckets full black tasting so good and felt so happy, that to eat them as like being in the church. Just one of the berries and you felt anointed" (136). The idea of bringing just freed blacks together by way of a feast brings out Baby Suggs qualities of sharing the joy with the community. "124, rocking with laughter, goodwill and food for ninety, made them angry. Too much they thought." (137)

Why none informed Baby Suggs of coming doom, maybe because the colored people disliked the excess. Like in *Sula*, the dead robins' rain and it proclaims something is ominous, similarly the grandmother sniffs the disapproval in the air. Morrison is one of the finest artists who evokes atmosphere, builds up ethos and readers feel it, perceive it and dread it, all at a time. The innermost thoughts unfold before the reader and we peep into Baby Suggs' mind:

> She accustomed to the knowledge that nobody prayed for her—but this free-floating repulsion was new. It wasn't

white folks—that much she could tell—so it must be colored ones. And then she knew. Her friends and neighbours were angry at her because she had overstepped, given too much, offended them by excess. (138)

When the school teacher arrived both Baby Suggs and Sethe saw them. The slave enters in the wood shed, Baby Suggs was standing stock-still. Stamp Paid was there in the wood pole with an axe. Sethe's 'thick mother-love' overwhelmed her. She wanted to kill all her children. She did not succeed in killing all but one, her two-year-old daughter, Beloved. Sethe's sheer courage to survive through slavery and getting out of it without Halle, her husband was a feat. How she loved her children, she renders to Paul D after eighteen years:

We was here. Each and everyone of my labbies and me too. I birthed them and I got me out and it wasn't no accident. I did that. I had help, of course, lots of that, but still it was me doing it; me saying, Go on, and Now. Me having to look out. Me using my own head. But it was more than that. It was a kind of selfishness I never knew nothing about before. It felt good. Good and right. I was big, Paul D, and deep and wide and when I stretched out my arms all my children could get in between. I was that wide. Look like I loved em more after I got here. Or may be couldn't love em proper in Kentucky because they wasn't mine to love. But when I got here, when I jumped down off that wagon—there wasn't nobody in the world I couldn't love if I wanted to. (162)

For Sethe, Paul D. is the man "who could walk into a house and the women cry." (17) After talking about her mother love again and again the subject would remain one. After her agonizing experiences of slavery at Sweet Home, it was:

Simple: she was squatting in the garden and when she saw them coming and recognized the school teacher's hat, she heard wings. Little hummingbirds stuck their needle beaks right through her headcloth into her hair and beat their wings. And if she thought anything, it was No. No. Nono. Nonono. Simple. She just flew. Collected every bit of life she had made, all the parts of her that were previous and fine and beautiful, and carried, pushed, dragged them through the veil, out, away, over there where no one could hurt them. Over there. Outside this place, where they would be safe. (163)

The white school teacher whom Sethe faced, "looked him dead in the eye, she had something in her arms that stopped him in his tracks. He took a backward step with each jump of the baby heart until finally there were none." (164) She relates to Paul D.: "I stopped him, . . . I took and put my babies where they'd be safe." (164) After a long time Paul D. realizes that he was wrong in believing Sethe, Halle's girl, as helpless woman. He saw "here Sethe was new. The ghost in her house didn't bother her for the very same reason a room-and-board witch with new shoes was welcome. This here Sethe talked about love like any other woman; talked about baby clothes like any other woman, but what she meant could cleave the bone. This here Sethe talked about safety with a handsaw. This here new Sethe didn't know where the world stopped and she began. Suddenly he saw what Stamp Paid wanted him to see: more important than what Sethe had done was what she claimed. It scared him." (164)

Sethe's worldview differs here from Paud D's. When Paul D. said, "Your love is too thick," Sethe gave her insight and said "Love is or it ain't. Thin love ain't love at all." (164) In a crisp, short dialogue Sethe tells Paul D, about her thick love and how she strove to be on her guard as far as her mother love was concerned about the safety of her loved ones:

"Yeah. It didn't work, did it? Did it work?" he asked,
"It worked," she said.
"How? Your boys gone your don't know where. One girl dead, the other won't leave the yard. How did it work?"

> "They ain't at Sweet Home. Schoolteacher ain't got em."
> "May be there's worse."
> "It ain't my job to know what's worse. It's my job to know that is and to keep them away from what I know is terrible. I did that." (164-65)

The above dialogue represents what Morrison wants—to be able to write highly marked, black language with black characters stee ped in black culture." (Verdelle 126)

Thus, what makes Morrison's works her own is the unique way in which she negotiates the constraining of a given critical or authorial power and ensures the participation of the reader in the experience of her novel. For her the "lore . . . Gossip . . . magic . . . [and] sentiment . . . Centralize and animate information discredited by the west." (Rao 93)

The novel raises many questions. Denver's loneliness when Paul D enters 124 as well as when Beloved possesses Sethe. Morrison creates a world of bygone era, yet alive in every bit and piece. The image of chokecherry tree on the back of Sethe and the countless such black "song of many thousands gone" keep alive the sufferings of the Afro-American people. Morrison has observed that scholarly studies of slavery have always seemed to her "too big and flat." They were like realistic novels that in trying to include all the facts missed the essence. She also believed that "by working within narrow limits" instead of broad ones, she might be able to do "something deep." The depth she is speaking is the depth of the human heart, "Sethe's heart, which in its misery contains the misery of the race" (Scruggs 186-87)

Beloved proclaims her passionate belonging to Sethe in surrealistic prose and verse. She also demands the reader's recognition of her presence and role as "too real to be Gothic." In an absorbing passage, as Rao observes, "dramatically asserting the reconciliation of Sethe and Beloved, individual past and history, repression and relief, Morrison invents a new voice out of a ghost and a dead past." At the end of this section, in a poetic chant, the memories and minds of Sethe, Denver and Beloved combine to make a mutual song of possession:

> I waited for you
> You are mine
> You are mine
> You are mine. (217)

Yet in the novel there is ultimate voice that is collective. It is that of the woman in the exorcism ritual toward the end of the novel. Its power lies in the sensation of sound and not in the logical meaning of the Logos.

> The women . . . stopped praying and took a step back to the beginning. In the beginning there were no words. In the beginning was the sound, they all know what that sound sounded like. (259)

Among all her works, *Beloved* does stand out as an unforgettable creation, which celebrates life of Afro-Americans through slavery with women at the centre. For long, no reader can forget the haunted house 124 on Bluestone Road with Sethe, Denver, Beloved and Baby Suggs. The charged images, poetic language, interspersed with several narratives to top it with strong bond of mother love leave a deep impression on the reader's mind.

NOTES

Walter Clemmons, "A Graveyard of Memories," *Newsweek* 110 (28 Sept. 1987), p. 75.

Toni Morrison, *Beloved* (London: Picador, 1988).

Payant, Katherine B. *Becoming and Bonding: Contemporary Feminism and Popular Fiction by American Women Writers* (Westport: Connecticut, Greenwood Press, 1993).

Rao, Raghavendra R.M.V. "In Search of an Authentic Voice: Toni Morrison's Beloved," *Indian Journal of American Studies*, VII, 23:2 (Summer) 1993, pp. 91-93.

Charles Scruggs, *Sweet Home: Invisible Cities in the Afro-American Novel* (Baltimore: John Hopkins University Press, 1993).

Verdelle, A.J. "Loose Magic: A.J. Verdelle Interviews Toni Morrison," *Double Take*, 13 (Summer), 1998, pp. 121-28.

The Theme of Marginality in Toni Morrison's *The Bluest Eye*

J. SALVE

The theme of marginality can be properly understood and explored only by understanding the meaning of the word 'Marginal'. According to the anthropologist Victor Turner: "Marginals are simultaneous members (by ascription, optation, self-definition or achievement) of two or more groups whose social definitions and cultural norms are distinct from and often opposed to one another. What is interesting about these marginals is that they often look to their group of origin, the so-called inferior group, for communitas and to the more prestigious group in which they aspire to higher status as their structural reference group."

The black characters in Toni Morrison's novel *The Bluest Eye* are marginals who strive to initiate themselves into the American society dominated by the racist whites. At the same time, these marginals try to hold on to the views of their own beauty and cultural worth. The novel is an account of the victimization of black people in general and black women in particular, in the American social order. It is the story of the damaging influence of white standards on the lives of black Americans, the marginalised. The source of this marginality is racism which makes the life of the black characters of the novel, vulnerable. These people have no autonomous individual self. They are the bearers of race consciousness. Thus, the novel talks about black identity and black self-concept.

The story is about a poor black girl called Pecola Breedlove. She believes that the contempt and brutality which she meets within the society around her has its roots in her ugliness, her blackness. She is obsessed because she knows that she cannot be beautiful like any other white girl. A white girl has blue eyes and blonde hair which make her beautiful and accepted in society. Pecola believes that if she gained blue eyes, her ugliness will disappear and she will gain the love and security which is desperately missing from her life.

Pecola is made to realise her ugly, black existence by the society around her. Her classmate named Maureen, a light-skinned girl, teases Pecola and her friends by calling them black and ugly. Pecola and her friends sink under the wisdom, accuracy and relevance of Maureen's remark. They were nicer, brighter too but still lesser than Maureen. The black sensibility makes them ask themselves—"What did we lack?" "What was the thing that made her beautiful and not us?" The things that they lacked were the blue eyes, white skin, blonde hair, the American standards of beauty accepted by both the whites and the blacks.

The black boys too harass Pecola over the colour of her skin and the sleeping habits of her father, a black adult. Though the same is true about their fathers, their contempt towards Pecola can be traced to the contempt for their own blackness. But their ignorance of this fact is smoothly cultivated over years. The hatred of the black boys for the black girl is the self-hatred induced by racism. The belief that black was not valuable or beautiful is a conviction even in the minds of blacks.

Pecola's experience at Mr. Yacobowski's shop speaks volumes for this. He being a white, is at a loss to see a black girl in his shop. Pecola sees a vacuum in his eyes and total absence of recognition and glazed separateness. His distaste is for her blackness. Junior, a black boy and his mother too treat Pecola with hatred. The mother drives Pecola away from her house: "Get out you nasty little black bitch. Get out of my house." In the process of imitating the ways of the white woman, Pauline, Pecola's mother, neglects Pecola. She, at the birth of Pecola, declares that she is an ugly child. Pauline showers her love and affection on her white employer's child whereas she scolds and slaps her own child.

Pecola's mother wants to identify herself with the white women by imitating their ways. She is a black woman who longs for beauty, romantic love, recognition and desire to live an ideal feminine life. Deprived of the same, she develops self-hatred. She tries to explore herself as central rather than marginal. Pauline hates the ugliness of her house, her daughter and herself. She becomes an ideal servant because that role fulfills practically all her needs. She compares the lovely house and the household things of her employer, Fishers, with her own and neglects her house, her children, her man. For her, life at Fishers is light, more delicate, more lovely. She has found beauty, order, cleanliness and praise at Fishers' residence. Power, praise and luxury are hers in this house. Pauline keeps this order for herself, and does not impose it on her children. She teaches her children fear of being clumsy, being like father, of not being loved by God: "Into her son she beats a fear of growing up, fear of other people, fear of life."

In Pauline we see an attempt of a black woman to alienate herself from her own community. In Pauline we also see a black woman struggling against social and economic hostilities stacked against her. But in spite of the limitations set by her family, society and race, she endeavours to live by female American standards. A self-conscious rebel is seen in Pauline.

Cholly, Pecola's father, an orphan, had always felt insecure and alienated as a child. He is rootless and in search of his self, his identity. The rape of Pecola by her father Cholly could be an attempt to recede to the days of his first love. His love towards Pecola changes to lust and rage as he remembers the incident of his first act of intercourse he was forced to perform in a flashlight by the whitemen: "Get on with it nigger," I said, "get on wid it. An make it good, nigger, make it good." Saying this the flashlight man laughed a laughter of contempt and scorn. In the end Cholly rapes Pecola. This unnatural rape is the distortion of his love for Pecola.

Pecola becomes victim of her parents's discontent. Her parents's self-hatred which is extended to their daughter has its roots in racial social order in America which is the source of marginality. Pecola yearns for love from her parents. But her parents are unable to provide the same as they themselves are spiritually depraved because of the social order of which they are a part. It is their unworthiness which prevents them from giving their children a sense of worth. Thus, Pecola and her parents's spiritual deprivation and search for identity is the search of a race under subjugation due to many years of misery and neglect and lack of means to come up. They resign themselves to their fate. Pecola experiences suffering at the hands of these negligent parents. They fail to provide identity and security which have been denied to them too, in American social conditions. The emptiness of their life and its negativity destroys their self-image and creates a self-hatred. As W. Lawrence rightly notes: "Morrison is concerned with the ontological structures and mythological thought systems that blacks develop to define and reinforce their definition of self and existence." Thus the hatred of the Breedlove family members for one another is the result of internalization of racist hatred.

Pecola attempts to change her fate by means of prayer—prayer for blue eyes, prayer for the bluest eyes. Each night without fail she prayed for the blue eyes. Pecola believed:

> If those eyes of hers were different, that is to say beautiful, she herself would be different. . . . If she looked different, beautiful maybe, Cholly would be different, and Mrs. Breedlove too. Maybe they would say. "Why, look at pretty-eyed Pecola. We mustn't do bad things in front of those pretty eyes."

Thus she believes that blue eyes could change everything. She will be loved by her people as well as by the whites, once her eyes turned blue. But unfortunately she becomes a victim of the racial culture. She is driven insane as she fails to meet the white standards of beauty, as she has been under the influence of white cultural domination.

Claudia Mcteer, who is Pecola's friend and also a black girl, tears apart a white doll which should be any girl's treasure. Her curiosity is to find out what makes the world appreciate and love white dolls with blue eyes, pink skin and blonde hair. Claudia tries to discover the source of beauty, whereas Pecola tries to become one by praying for bluest eyes. Morrison thus tries to explore the myth of standards of beauty of whites. Pecola falls a prey to the pressures of these traditional standards of beauty accepted by both the whites and blacks. K. Sumana says, "They are taught that their blonde hair, blue eyes and creamy skins are not only wonderful but are the surface manifestations of the very best character God and nature ever moulded. Oral traditions bolstered by literature and other media have solidified their pedestalization." The thrice-repeated primer serves as the prefatory material of the novel and also assists in unraveling the theme of racism. The first version of the primer is immediately repeated twice and is in simple language. "Here is the house. It is green. It has a red door." The second version has no spacing or punctuation. It is the lifestyle of two black Mcteer children Claudia and Frieda who are friends of Pecola. Their lifestyle is shaped by poor and loving parents who survive racism. The second version runs as:

HERE IS THE HOUSE IT IS GREEN AND WHITE HAS DOOR IT IS VERY PRETTY.

The third version is a run-on version which may mean the distorted lives of the Breedloves—Cholly, Pauline, Sam Pecola. These individuals fail to conform to the standards by which beauty and happiness are measured. This version seems to signify nothing. As Klotman points out: "First and foremost it serves as a synopsis of the tale that is to follow revealing the psychic confusion of the novel. It also serves as an ironic comment on a society which educated and unconsciously socialized its children like Pecola with callous regard for the cultural richness and diversity of its people."

The seasonal divisions of the novel as Autumn, Spring and Winter are a deliberate attempt to show the fundamental decadence of black Americans, the marginalised ones. The use of names of seasons aids Morrison in revealing the theme more effectively. Autumn suggests that the world of the novel is all distorted. The season divisions shed more light on the decadent lives of the blacks living in America.

The chapter which introduces us to the Breedlove family refers to Jane's very happy family.

> HERE IS THE FAMILY. MOTHER, FATHER, DICK AND JANE. THEY LIVE IN THE GREEN AND WHITE HOUSE.

But the family presented in the preceding chapters is just the antithesis of the standardised white family of the primer. It tells us about the black family of Breedloves whose members live a life of unhappiness and self-hatred. The bourgeois myth of ideal family life in America is exposed here. This myth does not apply to the lives of black Americans. These standards, on the contrary, bring barrenness and a sense of worthlessness, as experienced by Breedloves.

Though the novel is a study in race, gender and class, the main focus is on racism and its effects on the lives of Afro-Americans. Pecola suffers and is doomed because, she belongs to a black community, a marginalised group. Thus the novel exposes the devastating effect of racism on the self-image and psyches of Afro-Americans. It is a study of a people relegated to a class of marginals by virtue of their race. Racism serves as the source of this marginality. Whiteness is equated with beauty and culture and blackness with ugliness. The marginals too try to live by the values which the whites have created. Plackoottam rightly points out: "This covert form of racism was doubly injurious to the black race in that not much notice was taken of its invisibly corrosive nature."

BIBLIOGRAPHY

M. Awkward, *Inspiring Influences: Tradition, Revision and Afro-American Women's Novels* (New York: Columbia University Press, 1989).

Marie Evans, ed., *Black Women Writers (1950-1980), A Critical Evaluation* (Garden City, N.Y.: Anchor Press, Doubleday, 1984).

T. Harris, *Fiction and Folklore: The Novels of Toni Morrison* (Knoxville: University of Tennessee Press, 1991).

D. Samules and W.C. Hudson, *Toni Morrison* (Boston: Twayne, 1990).

C. Tate, ed., *Black Women Writers at Work* (New York: Continuum, 1983).

Towards a Minority Poetics:
A Critique of Binarism and Marginalism in Paule Marshall's Texts

HARIHAR KULKARNI

In keeping with the Derridean discourse of binarism and the Fanonian critique of "manichaeism delerium," Helene Cixous, in her 1981 *Signs* article entitled "Castration or Decapitation?" reminds that the patriarchal and colonial binary oppositions, "the protean imperialist form" as Benita Parry puts it, are a "violent hierarchy," which orders women, the colonized, and the marginalized culture as a deviant group socially and culturally. Such oppositions, where one of the two terms forcefully governs the other, where the primary sign becomes axiomatically privileged in the discourse of the colonial relationship, need to be subverted bringing low what was high, if women and the oppressed have to equip themselves with a capacity to decode the code of marginality and mystification, if those hegemonic, over-privileged, ever-signifying relationships are to be transformed into an aesthetics of balance and harmony. The political effects of ignoring this stage of subversion, of trying to jump beyond the hierarchy into a world quite free of it, is simply to leave it intact. In a way, it is also to corroborate the grain of status quo as ever before. Both the reversal of the authentic/inauthentic opposition and the subversion of authenticity itself are different aspects signifying topsyturvydom in a Derridean sense. Moreover, they are stages in a process of resistance.

Paule Marshall, the vanguardal, break through voice in the black feminist literary tradition of the Sixties, introduces such a process of resistance by evolving textual strategies in which the binarism of patriarchal and colonial hegemony is displaced or replaced by a different usage of the term. She exemplifies through these strategies that all the oppositions ultimately come back to mean that there exists negative value to the female/ black/ Third World, and positive value to the male/ white/ and the West side of opposition. "It is the classic opposition, dualist, and hierarchical. Man/Woman (black/ white) automatically means great/small, superior/inferior." (Cixous 1981: 5). Even Toril Moi (1985: 104) shares the same opinion when she comments: "Corresponding as they do to the underlying opposition man/woman (black/white), these binary oppositions are heavily imbricated in the patriarchal (colonial) value system, each opposition can be analyzed as a hierarchy where the 'feminite' (black) side is always seen as negative, powerless instance."

Marshall answers the question whether it is legitimate to use these oppositional paradigms developed in and for a Western context in order to analyze what could be called black feminist/ Third World literature.

This article attempts to make an inquiry into this possibility by analysing Marshall's second novel, *The Chosen Place, The Timeless People* (1969). Marshall often theorizes the need for replacing (a) text (b) language, and (c) theory as a strategy indispensable for the production of a distinct minority text, and redefining the idea of canonicity. In this particular novel she practises one of such strategies with which writing in *difference* at the level of text can be effected, with which the notion of legitimacy of patriarchal and colonial "imperialism of representation" can be chellenged and exorcized, and with which, as Barbara Johnson (1980: 5) puts it, "the claim to unequivocal domination of one mode of signifying over another" can be put to an end.

Inverting the world of hegemonic binary thought, Marshall makes implications not only to the feminist poetics but to the poetics of Minority literature as well. Though it could be argued that many of the characters in *The Chosen Place* are actually symbols for certain cultures of societal groups, they are nevertheless gendered and marginalized and an analysis based on gender relations can therefore be applied. The structure of the novel, arising as it does out of oppositions, is caught up within the framework of patriarchal binary thought which is subverted in a variety of ways. The opposition head/ emotions in the novel implies the reversed evaluation from that in the patriarchal pattern. The conflict between Merle Kinbona, and Harriet Shippen, for instance, is one example. Harriet, the WASP leader representing Western civilization, looks down on Merle, the central black woman in the novel because of the latter's continual outbursts of emotion which could be interpreted as a 'masculine' stance towards 'feminine' expressiveness, but later at the end of the novel it is just her inability to cope with emotions, instead of repressing the unpleasant, that contributes to her suicide, whereas Merle moves purposefully towards control and transcendence.

Also in another context, the contrast between Harriet and Merle can be seen as the reversal of a patriarchal convention. Their juxtaposition is in some ways reminiscent of the 19th century novelistic stereotype of opposing a 'dark' heroine to a 'fair' one. The dark woman is usually the more passionate, unrestrained, active, haughty one of the two, while the 'fair' woman is contained, passive, pure, Nordic. Often the plot does away with the 'dark' woman in some kind of way while the 'fair' woman heads for a happy survival. Merle is indeed the more unrestrained, emotional person of the two, and also the more active, independent, and haughty one. Harriet is more passive, eager to act as 'wife' prudish in sexual matters (234), and appears pure and untouched in sun and heat (175). In the opposition of those two, however, Harriet assumes the negative role and is the one who has to make way for Merle, the 'dark' woman. Here it is the 'fair' woman in an inversion of the 19th century pattern, who possess those qualities with negative values or lacks important qualities with negative values or lacks important qualities that are traditionally embodied by the 'dark' woman. Here, the novelist provides a pattern in which the axiologically fixed dichotomy construed by colonialist or patriarchal western thought, white/fair as sovereign law and black/dark as its transgression, with its attendant chain of naturalized antithesis, stands subverted. By disclosing the social and cultural positioning of the preconstituted and metaphysical poles of fair and dark, Marshall's writing is directed at liberating the consciousness of the oppressed from its confinement in the white man's artesian which operates existentially to deform the dialogical interaction of self with other selves, which proves detrimental to something that is essentially constitutive of and indispensable to authentic being and coterminous with consciousness.

The head/ emotion contrast is not only inverted with respect to its polarization of positive/ negative or superior/inferior, but also in its gender-specific distribution. In the juxtaposition of Harriet and Saul Amaron, it is Saul who is closer to emotion, while Harriet is equated with distance, control and the repression of emotion. Saul, for example engages repeatedly in intimate dialogue, sharing his experiences and facing unresolved emotional conflicts. Harriet is shown in direct verbal exchange much less often, her feelings and thoughts are related from an omniscient point of view and continues to be a distanced and detached character technically as well. Furthermore, she regularly smothers upcoming unpleasant emotions, suppressing them so as not to disturb her pre-established ordered world. Here then, it is the man who represents the 'feminine' quality of being emotional, while the woman stands for emotion control, repression and restraint—the qualities signifying masculine polarity.

The patriarchal gender-specific distribution of activity and passivity is also repeatedly inverted. In the scene where Vere and his new girl friend Milly, Elvita and Allen Fuso are seated together in Milly's room on a Carnival night, it is Elvita who actively pursues an encounter with Allen, who remains completely passive. He feels ashamed, however, of the role he plays in this encounter, as if it is not the role he is socially supposed to fulfill. Sexual energy or the lack of it are mostly symbolic of vitality or non-vitality, an opposition that goes with men/women in patriarchal society. Allen is neither able to be fulfilled emotionally, sexually with a woman nor to acknowledge his homosexual tendencies. But while passivity applying to a man, has a negative connotation here, it is nowhere implied that the woman should be passive.

Another occasion of the reversal of the activity/passivity pattern occurs when Cane Vale is shut down. Merle is the only character to act while all the men, the workers, stand in total passivity outside the factory gates, obeying the posted sign. (385) This is only one of the occurrences in which she ignores and subverts the patriarchal/ western order, symbolized here by the sign. In fact, to meet Merle Kinbona in the novel is to meet a hurricane power that sweeps the patriarchal or western power structure in reverse direction. It is Merle, a person steeped high in feminine power, who ignores all barriers of class and race, almost forcing everyone to acknowledge her and Bournehills (68, 71, 241). She cries, screams, drinks, smokes, smiles, laughs, jokes, nay drags everyone and everything along with her in her headlong race forward. But nearest her heart is Bournehills and its people. "She is the Queen, the primeval Goddess of the Island, a life-force, an earth mother who is the island, its past, present, and future." (Talmore 1987: 126) As opposed to men, Merle is "some larger figure, in whose person was summed up both Bournehills and its people." (260) She is the one who reverses the slave trade's triangular journey and goes to the cultural source so as to recontextualize the self that was decontextualized by white and patriarchal power of America. She is the one who traces the whole exploitative hierarchy from the base right upto the top, and it is she who realizes that nothing can be changed for people at the bottom of the heap if nothing is changed from the middle to the top. She is thus in opposition to the rules governing the exchange between different groups and races, partaking of all levels within the hierarchy and therefore questioning its validity, particularly as she engages in her own personal style of discourse with characters on all hierarchical levels.

As a female character and as the personification of the black/ Third World, she is set against the patriarchal western order. When, in her dealings with it which could be termed anarchic in its disregard of the rules of that order, she sees her limits and powerlessness as immediately after the Cane Vale episode, she retires completely through states of catatonia. With her it is either endless, anarchic talking or non-participation in that order. To this extent she is the character who is most effectively opposed to that patriarchal order. In the end, she is also the one character who is associated with activity, in bringing about a drastic change in her life. She sells almost all of her material possessions—though keeping the house—and makes ordering her emotional life her first priority. This also means a return to lover, her girl child being the symbol of the time in her life that had the potential for happiness, she gathers the strength to actively shape her future.

This leads us to one more significant facet of Paule Marshall's anti-patriarchal stance. Merle's union with her daughter in the novel is no mere coincidence but a textual strategy signifying yet another anti-patriarchal mode of representation. Reversing the father/son or even mother/son pattern of relationship commonly found in the Christian and Eurocentric doctrine and iconography which treats the mother-daughter relationship as the "dark continent of the dark continent," Marshall strikes chords of agreement with Helen Cixous and Luce Irigaray, who claim that the unsymbolized relationship between mother and daughter constitutes a veritable threat to the patriarchal symbolic order and its societal as well as cultural assumptions. Luce Irigaray argues: "The relationship between mother/daughter, daughter/mother constitutes an extremely explosive kernel in our societies. To think it . . . amounts undermining (ebranler) the patriarchal order." (Whitford 1991: 77)

The novel thus provides many instances where one finds an inversion of patriarchal binary association of the two poles of an opposition. The character Merle is particularly instrumental in this inversion. The novel's structure arising on binary oppositions, may not at times, be necessarily patriarchal in nature but these opposition can always run counter to the pattern established by patriarchal binary thought.

The novel also reveals that the Merle/ Harriet opposition can be logically reduced also to the opposition between the Third World and the West. Marshall (1973: 108) admits the novel's insistence on a vision "which sees the rise through revolutionary struggle of the darker peoples of the world and . . . the decline and eclipse of American and the West." Apparently on the one hand, there is the Third World, as represented by Bournehills, with its land exhausted and eroded, the sea wild and dangerous and the coast rocky. Its inhabitants are, for the most part, cane cutters and factory workers. Exploited perpetually, they live in poor conditions, part of them making a living as fishers or street sellers. However, they are queer people holding on to the past in their customs and folk tales. Equally strong is their dream of repetition of a revolt that took place centuries ago. They and their conditions are represented metaphorically by Merle Kinbona.

The West, on the other hand, is represented geographically by the Caribbean side of the island which, with its mild, soundless sea and beaches, is a vacation paradise for American tourists and expatriates who exploit the New Bristol youth sexually. The black bourgeoisie work in their interest, but is not accepted as equal. This bourgeoisie, in turn, emulates the Western middle class in its materialistic and "progressive" stance, favouring a capitalist modernization of the island. Its members live in big houses and look down on the peasantry, reminding them of their own heritage. The west exerts total economic control over Bourne Island through banks, businesses, and corporations, seen as an extension of the former colonial system. Embodied by Harriet, the West is portrayed as emotionally controlled and exact in organization while repressive of feelings. Marshall's juxtaposition of the Western world of colonial affluence and the Third World with its shacks, tiny plots and poverty sets both in relation to one another, illustrating how one group lives luxuriously because the other is poor, how the Bournehills people are 'yorked to a [Western] system that literally works them to death while it steals the fruits of their labor." (Christian. 1980: 113)

Marshall's textual strategies reveal that the Western code of living is essentially destructive, not only for the people who are subjected to it, but also for those who adopt it, such as Vere and his former girlfriend, and even for its proponents like Harriet. Fanonian idea of manichaeism delirium is drawn within sight as Marshall proceeds to subvert this binarism through a positive representation of the Third World embodied by the Bournehills society. Harriet dies because of her rigidly Western stance of distancing herself from other people and her inner life and because of her strife for dominance. "It is Harriet's inability to learn from Bournehills—it is her insistence on being useful on her own terms that finally leads to her undoing." (Christian. 1980: 123) Allan cannot find himself because he is trapped in irrationality and Merle overcomes her Western past, resolves the tormenting dilemmas and starts her life anew. The Bournehills people, despite their struggle for survival, regain the paradise of emotional equilibrium. They are aware of the oppression of their feelings about it in 'the Carnival' where they deal successfully with the contradiction between their dream and their actual living conditions in a mediated way which, as Frederic Jameson (1970: 162) puts it, "may be seen as a working out in formal terms of what a culture is unable to resolve concretely." Their enactments of the Pyre Hill revolt is nothing but their artistic expression both of a victorious past and promising future hopes. Indeed, the whole of the configuration of Third World/West opposition portrays a West destructive for both the oppressed and the oppressor and a Third World that holds in itself the strength to liberate itself and those willing to side with it.

In conclusion, it can be said that the novel's repetitive insistence on the reversal of the patriarchal and colonial binary thought testifies to Marshall's refusal of the categories of the white or male culture, its aesthetic, its illusory standards of normative or "correct" representation and its assumptions of a traditional and fixed meaning 'inscribed' in definitions. By directing attention to the disruptive articulations and acts of the colonized under patriarchy, or the west's cultural and representational hegemony, and by producing a text which is made to bear the burden of one's own cultural experience, Marshall, a pioneer in her own right in African-American women's literary tradition, subverts the concept of canonicity and presents the first imprints of a genuine minority discourse which, to use the words of Homi Bhabha (1986: 200), "is not simply the attempt to invert the balance of power within an unchanged order of the discourse, but to redefine the symbolic process through which . . . [a colonized] culture or community becomes 'subject' of discourse and 'object' of psychic identification."

A formulator of a Feminist and Third World aesthetic, Marshall offers highly discursive textual strategies which are both abrogate and appropriate at one and the same time and, in the process, provides new directions for writing in *difference* directions promoting the reconstruction of the canonical texts through alternative reading and writing practices which enact innumerable re-visionist assumptions about literature.

NOTES

Bhabha, Homi. 1986. "Difference, Discrimination, and the Discourse of Colonialism." In Gates: 189-204.
Christian, Barbara. 1980. *Black Women Novelists: The Development of a Tradition, 1892-1976*. Westport: Greenaroo Press.
Cixous, Helen, 1981. "Castration or Decapitation?" *Signs* 7, 1 (Autumn): 41-52.
Derrida, Jacques. 1972. *Positions*. London: Athlone Press.
Gates, Henry Louis, Jr. 1986. Editor. *Race, Writing and Difference*. Chicago: University of Chicago Press.
Jameson, Frederic. 1972. *The Prison-House of Language*. Princeton, N.J.: Princeton University Press.
Marshall, Paule. 1969. *The Chosen Place, The Timeless People*. New York: Harcourt Brace.
Marshall, Paule. 1972. "Shaping the World of My Art." *New Letters*. 40: 97-112.
Moi, Toril. 1985. *Sexual/ Textual Politics: Feminist Literary Theory*. New York: Methuen.
Talmor, Sascha. 1987. "Merle of Bournehills." *Durham University Journal*, 80, 1 (December): 125-128.
Whitford, Margaret. 1991. *Luce Irigaray: Philosophy in the Feminine*. New York: Routledge.